MULTIPLES IIIUMINATED

A collection of stories
and advice from parents of
twins, triplets and more

Edited by
Megan Woolsey and Alison Lee

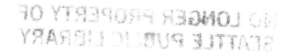

MULTIPLES ILLUMINATED

ISBN 978-0-99683-350-9

This book identifies product names and services known to be trademarks, registered trademarks, or service marks of their respective holders. They are used throughout this book in an editorial fashion only. In addition, terms suspected of being trademarks, registered trademarks, or service marks have been appropriately capitalized, although the authors cannot attest to the accuracy of this information. Use of a term in this book should not be regarded as affecting the validity of any trademark, registered trademark, or service mark.

Multiples Illuminated: A Collection of Stories and Advice by Parents of Twins, Triplets and More

Published 2016

CONTENTS

MULTIPLES
IIIUMINATED

A collection of stories
and advice from parents of
twins, triplets and more

FOREWORD

SUSAN PINSKY

Becoming a parent is one of life's defining experiences, but discovering that you're expecting multiples takes things to a whole new level. It is a time of excitement, anticipation, uncertainty and intense preparation. Even healthy couples with loving households and unlimited resources are going to be stressed and overwhelmed. Caring for human infants is difficult; caring for multiple children simultaneously is, well, intense.

Nowadays, multiple births are often the result of treatment for couples struggling with fertility issues. Dr. Drew and I were in this category. After much consideration we decided to embark on an odyssey that would result in a life-changing experience: raising triplets. The phenomenon of multiple births is an exciting and beautiful journey that can only be fully understood and appreciated if you have lived it firsthand.

Everything immediately changes upon learning that you are carrying more than one child. Not only does your pregnancy instantly become "high-risk," but then you and your partner are confronted with numerous issues that you've never even considered, let alone discussed.

In 1991, after our second round of in vitro fertilization, Drew and I learned that we were finally going have a baby. No, *babies*—lots of them. Ten days after we received positive results, we were at one of the many doctor's appointments that are the norm for complicated pregnancies. With my feet in stirrups and my husband by my side, the doctor embarked on a fishing expedition (with an internal ultrasound wand) to discover how many tenants I had in my uterus.

Hearing your child's heartbeat for the first time is undoubtedly an experience that is beyond compare. The effect of seeing FOUR tiny heartbeats is something else altogether. The thrill of having achieved a viable pregnancy is suddenly imbued with confusion, befuddlement, and abject fear.

"Say what?!?" I mustered, full of disbelief. The prospect of four babies growing inside me was confounding, as was the thought of the sudden loss of my youthful figure.

My overachieving workaholic husband, a physician himself, wasn't doing much better. "Jeez, how am I going to pay for four college educations *all at once*?" was about all he could manage, as he stood there, shell-shocked. He'd just read an article in the waiting room about college tuition predictions for the year 2011—bad timing to say the least. Maybe *that* should have been the required reading material when he was alone in the room with the cup a few weeks prior!

Needless to say, paying for college was not my primary focus at that moment. I was slightly more preoccupied with practical concerns like: HOW THE HELL WILL WE MANAGE WITH FOUR INFANTS? Slightly farther down the list was concern about my uterus' ability to accommodate all of them *simultaneously*. Then it dawned on me: this is all Drew's fault. WHAT HAS HE DONE TO ME? I had come from a middle-class family where merely looking at a guy could get you pregnant. As such, I'd spent my entire adult life avoiding this situation at all cost. Now I was on the verge of an insta-family of six!

With that, the roller coaster ride began.

Right after receiving the shock of our lives, we were confronted with the first of many delicate issues we would be forced to consider during this unique pregnancy: selective reduction. This is the cruel irony of in vitro fertilization: one day you can't get pregnant, and the next you're faced with the possibility of having to terminate one (or more) of your hard-won fetuses for health reasons.

Our obstetrician dutifully delivered his version of the patented speech about selective reduction, featuring all the medically compelling reasons to reduce from four fetuses to two.

The gravity of the decision whether to selectively reduce weighed heavily on us. I had five embryos implanted initially, and four of them had taken. Drew and I needed to evaluate whether we were comfortable with this scenario, and spent the next few weeks weighing the pros and cons of both options at a little getaway weekend where we were married.

At the next doctor's appointment, however, we learned that another one of the embryos hadn't survived. A revelation like this is met with sorrow and relief, but three babies suddenly seemed more manageable and we counted our blessings. Little did we know that the pregnancy would be the *easy* part.

I gave birth to our triplets on November 11, 1992, on Armistice Day. Douglas weighed in at six pounds, nine ounces, Jordan was five pounds, eight ounces and Paulina was an even five pounds. My hospital room was full of babies and flowers. It seemed that all of Pasadena had sent bouquets to welcome our children into the world as gorgeous arrangements filled my room and trailed down the halls of the maternity ward.

Unfortunately, I woke up feeling less than stellar as I reeled in pain and was not expecting the widespread attention of the entire city of Pasadena. Hence, my mood didn't always match the loveliness I beheld in my hospital room during those first days as a mom. Sore from the extraction of three babies, and having come close to death during their dramatic arrival was tough enough without Drew repeatedly announcing that my uterus "was now the size of Wisconsin." In an instant any career objectives I may have harbored were silenced; I was destined to be a stay-at-home mom, landlocked in Pasadena for at least the next 18 years.

When the kids were about three months old, it didn't help that my girlfriends never invited me to lunch with their singletons, or that I was constantly besieged with questions from the general public who stared at my brood and me like we were a novel form of entertainment. Often during these outings I had to remind myself that I was the luckiest woman in the world. The benefits of modern science had given me three beautiful, healthy, bald children. I told myself that if I had to endure the same annoying questions a thousand times, it would still be worth it because I had my three precious peace-givers.

Despite the fact that I was raised in a household where stereotypical gender biases were the norm, I made a conscious effort **not** to impose them on my children. I considered myself liberated from outdated ideas about how girls and boys were expected to look or behave. In college I studied the question of nature versus nurture, and embraced the perspective that gender roles were nothing more than constructs of society. Given opportunity and freedom of choice, children did not necessarily have to conform to traditional roles assigned to them by society.

To that end, and as a test of my perspective, we had a social experiment and tried to avoid traditional toys that were considered "gender specific" in our house. We focused on activities involving potty training, books, and music videos. I was very proud of our efforts and was curious if our children would be unaffected by the environment in which they were raised, and how they would react when exposed to conventional attitudes about gender.

One day, when they could all walk unassisted, we decided to take them to the toy store. After unloading them from the ever-conspicuous triplet stroller, we watched as they skipped joyfully into this new mecca of toy-dom, unfettered and free to explore whatever interested them.

Even at this tender age, they had very distinct tastes and personalities. We were excited to see where their interests would lead them. We refused to flinch if one of the boys liked feather boas, and we would wholeheartedly support Paulina if she chose a pirate ship over a Barbie doll. But none of that happened. Squealing with delight, Paulina went straight to the section of dolls and princess accessories, and the boys were immediately drawn to the cars, trains and tools. We tried to drag her away to be with the boys, and vice versa, to no avail.

I grew up in the pre-Caitlin Jenner era. My generation was rarely exposed to different interpretations of gender roles, and yet, here I was conducting a case study on my children. What I learned is that, despite all reasonable efforts to the contrary, gender bias is not environmental, and nearly unavoidable. More often than not, girls do not get programmed to like dolls via our rewards, and boys don't learn to like cars. It's not up to us to decide. They know innately. We were open to that.

The important thing with multiples is to help them excel in what interests them individually. This is the part that's hardwired and where genetics come into play. All three of my children had the same lessons and activities during their childhoods, yet they have wildly divergent interests as adults. Douglas is a singer and accomplished piano player who sings opera (like his father). Paulina, who figure skated competitively, is pursuing a career in comedy writing, and Jordan, who loved working on the computer solving math problems on Millie Math House when he was two, graduated with a degree in advanced mathematics and has Drew's photographic memory.

Their shared upbringing resulted in them having lots of similarities and even more differences. They all recently graduated from top institutions. Their grade point averages were similar throughout their educations, but they all earned different degrees. I could not be prouder of their achievements, and Drew and I will support them unfailingly as they strive for their next set of goals. Oh, and we were able to figure out how to pay the entire bill by saving money along the way.

As parents of triplets, we endeavored to instill strong values, self-confidence, and impeccable work ethic. We wanted them to do their best and be good, loving people as they pursued their individual interests. Mission accomplished.

However, it wasn't all easy.

A weekend getaway to Las Vegas with my husband and the thirteen-month-old trio was the beginning of a harrowing chapter in our family's life. While taking a break in the hotel room after a long day, Douglas decided it would be fun to jump on the bed. After a few seconds of gleeful bouncing, I watched in horror as he catapulted himself off the bed and slammed headfirst onto the floor. I launched toward him, anticipating the screams that were sure to follow such a hard impact. Silence. Fortunately, I had just read an article in *Parents* magazine about childhood head injuries and recognized that his lack of reaction was serious.

We dialed 911 and watched helplessly as the paramedics worked on Douglas, who had no pulse. Overcome with guilt and terror, Drew and I piled into the ambulance with our baby, who was immobilized with a neck brace but alive. I sobbed uncontrollably as I sang "A Spoonful of Sugar" to him repeatedly all the way to the hospital.

It was eerily silent as we sat in the waiting room for what seemed like an eternity. Finally, we heard him cry. The room filled with his operatic wailing, and it was the best sound we'd ever heard. But we weren't going to get off that easy.

Douglas' CAT scan revealed a large dark spot on his brain, diagnosed as an arachnoid cyst. Arachnoid cysts are sacs of cerebrospinal fluid that result from developmental abnormalities that occur during early gestation. Douglas' cyst was located in his cerebellum, the area of the brain that controls balance. His surgery was scheduled for the following week.

Having triplets on your first foray into parenting is incredibly overwhelming when everything is going right. Discovering that one of your babies is in a life-threatening situation that will require years of medical treatment increases the stress level exponentially. Douglas' surgery went well, but it came with collateral damage, including subsequent bouts of depression. The feeling of heartbreak at hearing your child say, "No one cares if I live, Mama," is indescribably excruciating.

Multiples are subject to many disabilities and developmental problems associated with low birth weight. The stigma of dealing with mental health issues is difficult for anyone—especially for a child. We were fortunate to have access to an exceptional neuropsychologist who helped us learn how to cope with the aftermath of Douglas' brain surgery. We learned to implement techniques that helped his development and improved his behavior, which was previously misdiagnosed as "willfulness." This was a challenging process for Drew and me, as well as our other two children.

The incredible experience of having triplets tested our limits at times, but we survived. When Douglas graduated from college, he cut his hair, revealing the scar on his head for the first time in his twenty-two years. He posted a photo in his cap and gown with a quote that said:

"To the ones who have had surgeries, broken bones, mental illness; to the ones who were called slow or were left unheard; you can compete, and you can make a difference. Congratulations, Vanderbilt Class of 2015. You picked up a fighter when he almost gave up on his dreams and proved that passion can reverse adversity."

Back when I learned I was having triplets, resources for parents of multiples was extremely limited. *Parents* magazine was my go-to source for everything. The Internet, as we know it, was in its infancy, and support group attendance relied primarily on word of mouth—support groups I had zero time to attend in the first place. Being a parent of multiples has the potential to be a very frustrating, lonely and isolating experience.

Nowadays, with the click of a button, one can be in touch with any number of people who are experiencing the infinite joys and challenges of raising multiples. *Multiples Illuminated* is a fantastic resource that provides wonderful advice and information for all parents, and it is a *priceless* resource for parents who are faced with the incredible and unique experience of raising multiples. We are only human, and we make mistakes, but we can accomplish amazing things through the trials and tribulations we experience. Parents of multiples are blessed, and must celebrate the beautiful lives we have created—whether it's one, two, three, four, or even more, at a time!

Susan Sailer Pinsky is the mother of triplets who all recently graduated from top colleges. She is the creator and CEO of Playroom Podz, the podcast provider for "This Life," with Dr. Drew and Bob Forrest. She is also the producer and host of "Calling Out with Susan Pinsky," which features the world's best psychics as well as celebrity guests. Her show is one of iTunes most popular podcasts focusing on psychic phenomena. In 2015 she was the recipient of the LA Music Award for "Best Radio Host." In addition to running her podcast company, Susan works tirelessly behind the scenes to promote her husband's brand, employing her marketing skills to publicize DrDrew.com and the very popular Dr. Drew podcast.

Susan and Drew have been married for 25 years, having met in 1984 when she was a guest on his successful radio show, "Loveline." As such, she is known to her Twitter and Instagram followers as @Firstladyoflove.

No stranger to the red carpet, Susan has accompanied her famous husband to many glamorous Hollywood events over the years. She also appeared with him on the hit television show "Legit." She loves the world of beauty and has been a judge for the Miss Nevada, USA pageant for the past two years.

Susan is passionate about philanthropy and serves on the Board of Hillsides in Pasadena. During her tenure, the organization has raised several million dollars to help children in need throughout the greater Los Angeles Basin.

Susan currently resides in Pasadena with her husband, her oldest triplet, and two adorable Australian shepherds.

FOREWORD

INTRODUCTION

MEGAN WOOLSEY AND ALISON LEE

Multiples have been a source of fascination for years, and the increase in the number of twins, triplets and more being born year after year certainly hasn't dissipated that interest. Nowadays, there are numerous television shows about multiples, such as *In the Womb*, exploring the extraordinary and fragile journey of multiples beginning at conception; *Twinsters*, a documentary about identical twins who were separated at birth and found each other in adulthood; *The Secret Life of Twins* and *Two of a Kind* both look at how nature and nurture play their parts in the lives of multiples; and a two-part British documentary called *The Triplets are Coming* looks at the ins and outs of treating and caring for mothers pregnant with triplets.

However, a quick scan of the shelves in a bookstore is less impressive. Compared to generic reading material for new and expectant parents, parents of multiples have fewer choices. Whether you were pregnant with triplets eight years ago, or with twins a year ago, or midway through pregnancy now, the number of quality and helpful books about what life is like expecting, birthing and caring for multiples, is scarce.

When Megan was only eight weeks pregnant with triplets, she was filled with fluctuating emotions. One day she was ecstatic that her heartbreaking years of infertility were finally over, the next day she was scared about how she would take care of three babies at once. Some days she was proud that she would be a mom of multiples, the next she was awake in the middle of the night worrying that she would never get to travel outside her town again.

Being pregnant with multiples is a challenging experience. It's beautiful and exciting, yet also terrifying and a test of physical endurance. The huge belly. The pressure on the chest when lying down. The kicks and jabs on all parts of your belly, chest and pelvis. The enormous appetite, yet the lack of space in the stomach. The very real fear of preterm labor and the possibility of a NICU stay for the babies. All the concerns, pains and aches of pregnancy are multiplied.

The questions also multiply: How will I deliver two/three/four babies? What will the NICU experience be like? How will I breastfeed more than one baby? Will I ever sleep again? How will I care for the twins/triplets/quads? Will I have help?

Newly pregnant women have many questions, and they can usually find answers in books. Newly pregnant women with twins/triplets/quads have even more questions and find themselves floundering for information, support and help. We want to be excited, but the unknown creeps up like a cold breeze on a hot summer day. People usually do not know what to say to us.

With a lack of knowledge about carrying and raising multiples, we began searching for answers. We scoured the Internet looking for books to teach us about raising multiples. Megan taped every show she could find on the Discovery Channel about multiples. Eight years ago there was not enough good information, but she bought everything she could find (five books in total).

There is one humorous book, *I Sleep at Red Lights,* written by Bruce Stockler about his experience with infant triplets that is a fun and enjoyable read. However, there isn't a single book with beautifully written stories that would give mothers of multiples hope and inspiration, and offer relatable information to arm themselves in this new and exciting, yet lonely and scary world.

We conceived *Multiples Illuminated* to shed light (see what we did there?) on the world of raising multiples. How we would have appreciated a book like *Multiples Illuminated* when we were pregnant with our multiples, wondering what life would be like for us.

We wanted to write this book to offer the parents of multiples around the world something delicious to indulge in. There are words of wisdom and personal stories that we hope will inspire you and make you proud to be a part of the world of multiples.

If you read *Multiples Illuminated* and feel optimistic, inspired, informed, and connected about raising multiples, we have done our job. We are creating a community of parents who need to think outside the box to successfully raise two or more children simultaneously.

In this book are stories that will make you laugh, and stories that will make you cry, sprinkled with helpful advice and journal prompts for you to tell your own heart's story.

Thank you for trusting us to join your multiples adventure; we hope these stories illuminate you.

Megan and Alison
Editors

INTRODUCTION

PERMISSION GRANTED:
A POEM DEDICATED TO NEW MOTHERS
OF MULTIPLES

MEIMEI FOX

It's okay not to floss or
wash your face and
let the mascara cake on your eyelashes and
run down your cheek like
a circus clown.
It's okay to not
put on any makeup at all.

It's okay to fantasize about going
to the grocery store
just so you can stand
in the produce aisle and
pretend to be the same old you.

It's also okay not to go to the store, or
even leave the house.
To order in pizza and eat cereal
for dinner
every night
for a week straight
(which would have horrified you only
months before.)

It's okay to forget things you never
used to forget like
where you put your car keys or
your mother's birthday.
It's okay not to open your mail or
pay your bills for a while.
To lose track of the day, the week and
to make mistakes
drop the ball.

It's okay not to breastfeed and
not explain, justify, or apologize for why. And
it's also okay to breastfeed yet
lament your poor, chapped nipples. And
it's also okay to pump
because it's more convenient.

It's okay to miss your breasts being sexual,
to bemoan how you've become
A milk truck.

It's okay to loathe your body,
to resent its invasion by aliens who
ballooned out your ass and
turned your waistline into a tree trunk and
injected your abs with silly putty.

It's okay to envy those "fabulously fit!"
new mom Hollywood stars with
their personal chefs and trainers.
(Damn them.)

It's okay to go back to work because
you have to,
even though you hate it, or
because you want to because
it makes you feel sane. And

it's also okay if you choose to be a full-time
stay-at-home mom but
worry it will undermine your self-esteem. And
it's okay to feel ambivalent, resentful, sad
at times
whatever reality you face.

It's okay to fight with your partner like
you have never fought before --
meaner, uglier --
lashing out at him for not
doing as much as you do, for not
grabbing that baby out of your hands
the minute he walks in the door, for
doing a better job than you do, of
taking care of himself, his needs.
It's okay to worry that your babies
have ruined your relationship forever.

It's okay to become a neurotic mess,
checking your babies' breathing
15 times in the night.
It's okay to feel that you are not
maternal enough, not
wise enough, not
capable enough, not
patient enough, not
enough.

Not enough. And
to wonder who the hell
put you in charge
anyway.

It's okay to cry,
to sob soul-shaking, heaving
moans of despair,

to think, "What have I done?"
To feel convinced that you have
ruined everything
only now there is no going back.

It's okay not
to be perfect
or even anywhere close,
to feel disappointed in yourself,
depressed,
and flat out fatigued like
you're being held underwater by a tidal wave
and will never get to come up for air.

It's okay because
the first three months, or maybe six, or
maybe longer
you're in a fox hole and
it's World War 3 and
even if you're not alone, you sometimes feel
you are and
the bombs are exploding all around you –
Bang! Bang! Bang!
and the babies are screaming they need
to be fed, they need
to be changed, they need
you, and you,
you are sleep deprived beyond comprehension and
overwhelmed as you
experience the most profound transformation of your
lifetime
(aside from your *own* birth and death).

It's okay because
this too shall pass.
Everything is temporary.
Your feelings will come and go.

Your frustrations – and joys –
will arise and subside,
only to be replaced by others . . .
like waves crashing on the shore.

It's okay because you won't become a mother overnight—
but
you *will* become a goddess over time.

It's okay because
there will come that moment -- the one
you have read about and heard
your friends talk about and
dreamed of the whole of your pregnancy or
maybe your entire life -- when
you will gaze into your babies' eyes and feel
sigh
feel so . . .
in love. So
content. So
complete. So
certain that
you are exactly where you want to be.
These are the beings who chose you, and
you are beyond blessed. You
may well be
the luckiest woman in the world.
Yes, that moment will come.

It's okay because,
whether we talk about it or not,
we all struggle,
we all doubt,
we all drown. Especially when
there is not one baby but
two. Or

three. Or . . .
Wow. And
no one who has had just one baby
at a time
will ever fully comprehend
our experience.

It's okay because
for us mothers,
for our babies,
for our world and all humanity,
there is
no one way
no best way
no right way. There is
only your way.
Only the way that works for you and
your babies and
your tiny budding rose blossom of
a world.

And the only way to get there, the only way
to bloom into the stunning flower that
you are, that
your babies are,
is by being
Here
Now
with whatever it is that
is arising and
accepting it
as so.

Permission granted.

MeiMei Fox is a New York Times bestselling author who publishes her own daily blog, Adventures with Twins. She contributes regularly to The Huffington Post, MindBodyGreen, among other publications. MeiMei also works as a life coach, assisting clients in realizing their most ambitious dreams. She graduated Phi Beta Kappa with honors and distinction from Stanford University, with a BA and MA in psychology. MeiMei lives in Hawaii with the Love of Her Life, her husband Kiran Ramchandran, and their twin boys. Her mantra is Fear Less, Love More!

INTRODUCTION

INFERTILITY AND TRYING TO CONCEIVE

SURVIVING INFERTILITY
AND TRYING TO CONCEIVE

MEGAN WOOLSEY

I had my first child without the help of fertility treatments, but it took me a year and a half to conceive. During that time, I suffered an ectopic pregnancy where the embryo left my entire reproductive system and attached to the bladder.

Two years after my daughter was born, I suffered two miscarriages in a row, one exiting my body naturally and the other requiring surgical intervention. Both were physically and emotionally painful.

I visited a fertility doctor who gave me a battery of tests and determined that I had "diminished ovarian reserve." This meant that at the youthful age of 32 I was no longer producing good quality, viable eggs. The fertility doctor looked at me with his less than desirable bedside manner and said in a flat tone that I would never be able to have any more children with my eggs. I had two choices: pay $20,000 for a donor egg or fork up a minimum of $10,000 to adopt a child.

I was crushed with thoughts of never having any more children. The natural process of reproduction that seemed to come remarkably easily for the friends and family around me was now out of reach for me. I agonized over never experiencing another pregnancy, delivery or holding a new baby again.

Yet, I couldn't shake the feeling that it would be possible to have children with my own eggs again. If I was still producing eggs, did diminished ovarian reserve mean that I didn't have a single good egg left? Just two years earlier I had conceived my daughter with my very own inferior eggs.

I took my fertility testing results and emailed them to the doctors at another fertility clinic. They thought I had a chance of getting pregnant and were willing to help me.

For months, I stabbed my belly with needles of liquid containing hormones and blood thinners as I moved through the in vitro fertilization (IVF) process. They inserted wands, retrieved eggs and placed them in petri dishes.

It was beautiful. I was hopeful.

The first two cycles failed. On the third IVF cycle we decided to put four great looking embryos in because I just could not bear to come out of this without a baby. Six weeks later, Chris and I learned in the ultrasound room of the clinic that three babies had successfully fertilized. I watched in disbelief as three hearts beat with fervor inside my belly.

When a doctor tells you that you will never have another baby with your own eggs, do not take their words at face value. Do your own research. Get second and third opinions. Doctors do not know everything about what is going on inside your body.

Tips on Surviving Fertility:

• Always get a second opinion.

• Discuss with your partner how long you are willing to undergo fertility treatments.

• There are a lot of needle pricks during the process of trying to conceive, but it will become less dreadful as you get used to it (I ended up giving myself all of my own shots during the IVF process).

- If you have other children, line up a readily available babysitter because there are countless appointments that you aren't going to want to bring children to.

- Don't dismiss alternative therapies while going through fertility treatments, like acupuncture, yoga or meditation. I tried acupuncture during the cycle that ended in triplets.

- Share details of your fertility treatments wisely: only share with a select group because it is an emotional time for you, and people tend to say the wrong thing.

- Women going through infertility treatments bear the brunt of the physical discomforts, but don't forget that it is an emotional process for both partners and it's important to care for each other.

- It's okay to cry it out—undergoing fertility treatments will test your will.

- Exercise—it is helpful if your body is in a healthy condition for the taxing times to come.

- Quell the jealousy you feel towards friends and family who are pregnant. Pregnancy comes easier for them, but other things in life may come easier for you.

- The process of trying to conceive is grueling and not always fun, but it is making you tougher and stronger. Embrace it!

- Forgive yourself. It isn't your fault.

Infertility is heartbreaking for everyone involved. Don't lose hope. Modern medicine affords us a second chance. Stay strong through the journey, and good luck.

EGG-OTISM

SHELLEY STOLAROFF SEGAL

Pregnancy is fun (most of the time) but infertility, not so much. When I tried to conceive 25 years ago, I had to field well-worn lines like, "Thank God you're only in your 30s. Did you know you're less likely to get pregnant after 40 than getting struck by lightning?" I had to fake thank all the well-meaning people I knew who cut out every magazine and newspaper article they could find to educate me about infertility. Like I didn't know anything. You know, like it was all news to me.

I just wanted to go through the beauty and humiliation of conception alone (and perhaps with my husband, Jeff). However, it wasn't to be. I couldn't battle the power of the grapevine. The results of our sperm tests were public. Everyone knew about the state of my follicles. The entire planet pondered over which drugs, prayers, science, and voodoo had taken hold of my body that month. I'm not complaining, really I'm not. My friends and family, and their friends and family, and their friends and family, were very supportive. I guess it does take a village to raise a fertilized egg. When I look back, I truly appreciate the level of absurdity I reached to get pregnant.

It started with my grandmother-in-law's suggestion to put a dime between my teeth and throw my legs into the air for 40 minutes after a rendezvous. A romantic tryst. You know, one of those sultry science projects you carefully chart and schedule two weeks ahead of time. "I'm sorry, Grandma, it didn't work." "What? You must've done it wrong!" No, there are only a few ways to stick a dime in your mouth. And for 40 minutes? I'm just glad I didn't choke.

Then it was my mother's turn. She knew how much I was struggling, so on one occasion when she came to visit me— we were living in Indiana at the time—she handed me a handkerchief she'd brought from Texas that was anointed with holy oil from her housekeeper's church. This was going to work; she just knew it. She whispered, "Shelley, you're supposed to place this on your face when you and Jeff are..." Stop right there. It was bad enough that I had to wear a hankie during sex but to discuss it with my mother was too much. The advice didn't matter anyway because the handkerchief did not work. All it did was make me laugh and sneeze. Very sexy.

I dabbled in fertility drugs for years. I'll never forget my first experience shooting up. I used to do Lupron before bedtime. My sweaty hand would shake as I held it over my thigh, but after a while I grew accustomed to the protocol knowing that it may literally bear fruit one day. I never smiled when I jabbed myself though, unlike my husband who smirked every time he stuck me in the bottom with a needle that looked more like a bicycle pump. He shot me up with Pergonal every night. And before the draconian stab I'd call my mother for support. "Mom, are you there?" I would lay the phone down on the bed, bend over, count to three, and let Jeff have his way with me. Mother would listen to me scream and then validate the horror of it all. But alas, the drugs didn't work either. Or the turkey basting. Or anything. I was still as barren as Sarah.

Eventually, I ran all of the bases with no home run. I felt like a loser. A desperate loser. And the cocktail of drugs I was taking didn't make me feel any better. Sometimes at night I would leave our bedroom and just pace the house. "Something is wrong with me. Something is wrong with my body." It was hard to feel positive when no one could explain my "unexplained infertility." I thought it was strange that we could send people to the moon, or perhaps to even Mars one day, but we couldn't figure out the "follicularly-challenged."

Science and religion hadn't been productive, so to speak. I had to try something radical. I needed magic. I visited a friend in Massachusetts, an hour away from Salem, a bewitching city steeped in history. I wasn't feeling super or natural, but I was running out of options. I demanded that she drive me there. Once we arrived, I combed the streets until I found a provocative-looking shop. I entered the store flushed and hormonal. When one of the women in black asked if she could help me, I blurted out, "I can't get pregnant!" And then I cried. Well, this turned out to be a pretty famous place (like the kind you see on The Travel Channel), and this very helpful professional (who looked like Glenda from *The Wizard of Oz*, but with raven hair) took care of me. To this day, I'll never know if it was the bottle of divine purpose oil she gave me that did the trick, or if it was the conversation I had with God in my closet the night before my IVF procedure: "Well, it's come down to the wire, and I don't have to conceive tomorrow if You don't think it's a good idea. I have lots of plans and goals that don't revolve around children. I'm excellent at being self-involved, so maybe I should stay that way. Anyway, I'm turning this over to You now. If it's meant to be, if I'm meant to be a mother, then I will go with it and be happy. But if it doesn't happen, I'll be okay."

When I got the call a few weeks later, I sat down on my bed staring at my friends' gaping mouths, trying to process the information and its ramifications. I was going to have a child! The hard work and humiliation paid off. My teeth started chattering. It was all meant to be. Shock and elation. And then more shock and elation, a few months later. "Oh my God, Mom, I'm going to have twins! TWINS. Can you believe it? Twins?!" I could practically hear her gagging on the other line. Later, when we learned it was going to be a boy and a girl, I was shocked, elated, and giddy. Jeff was thrilled. So were our friends and family. And their friends and family.

After five years of getting pulled over by the cops while dashing to and from fertility clinics. After five years of scrambled eggs and hyper-stimulated emotions. After five years of incredibly embarrassing moments with my mother-in-law, neighbors and friends. After five years of painful procedures, dashed hopes and hysterics…I was pregnant. Not with one test tube miracle, but two. I like to tell people that my tall, leggy fertility doctor was the father of my children. And I'm happy to report that my Titanic twin pregnancy WAS fun. But that's a story for the next book…

Shelley Stolaroff Segal is a playwright, actor, composer, and essayist living in Greensboro, NC. My Son, *her play about autism and race, premiered in NYC and was presented as a TED talk at TEDx East. Her non-fiction essays and articles have been published in the books,* Voices from the Spectrum, Cup of Comfort/Autism, Chicken Soup for the Soul, *and the magazine,* Autism/Asperger's Digest.

INFERTILE IN A PREGNANT WORLD

SHANNA SILVA

We all make deals. Sometimes we trade to get things we want. Other times, from a deep, desperate place, in our silent pleading, we promise that if we can get what we want, we will change our fundamental selves and innate behaviors. Sometimes these promises are the only means of control we have left.

Lying on the x-ray table with a speculum inserted, the lab tech passed a tube of contrast dye through my uterus and fallopian tubes. I gingerly shifted into different positions as films of my reproductive organs were recorded. The results of this hysterosalpingogram could show an anatomical abnormality or blockage that prevented conception.

If I can get pregnant, I will be a better wife/daughter/ sister.

After my husband and I had been married for a couple of years, we decided to have children. In my mind, this would happen quickly after ending birth control, and I was shocked that I didn't become pregnant within the first few months. As if to highlight our infertility, I noticed pregnant women everywhere and wondered why my body was failing me.

After six months without success, we sought medical intervention from my gynecologist. We stared at the pregnant bellies in the waiting room and hoped for a simple solution. Instead of taking our concerns seriously, the doctor told me to "have a drink or two and just relax." He offered no therapeutic insight and did no testing. We were dismissed and made to feel neurotic. Trying to heed the "professional" advice, I attempted to relax. But relaxing on command only creates more stress. My first conscious thought each morning was about getting pregnant, and it shadowed me throughout the day. It was all I wanted to talk about, as if my constant attention and verbalization would make a difference and change the reality. I was obsessed.

It occurred to me a year into the drinking-but-not-relaxing process that my doctor was a moron. How did he know there wasn't something wrong with one of us? He had done nothing to validate or refute that a medical problem existed. We needed real help.

After some research, we went to see an infertility specialist, hopeful that we were on the right path. The office was decorated tastefully, with serene colors and parenting magazines neatly stacked on the tables. One wall was covered with baby photographs, sprawling over the bulletin board like roots of a tree. I imagined a picture of my child hanging on the wall, offering hope to other infertile couples.

We became willing lab rats in a roster of science experiments. The team of doctors tested many theories: bad eggs, slow swimming sperm and a sperm allergy that could cause my body to produce sperm antibodies. Every test was negative. We fell into the category of "unexplained Infertility." They had no idea why we weren't conceiving, or if we ever would. We were medical mysteries. Had there been a specific problem, there would be a defined medical solution. Instead, we had a vague defective label and several paths to ponder and select.

How could I be infertile? I'd done nothing to deserve it. My husband and I could provide a loving home and wonderful advantaged life to a child. The news was full of stories of teenage girls giving birth secretly at school dances to unwanted babies that they discarded like last season's prom dress. If anyone deserved infertility, it was them.

Fix our unexplained infertility and I will be more charitable.

We began the process of artificial insemination. I took the drug Clomid to produce multiple eggs and provide additional targets for sperm. Each day, I recorded my temperature on a chart, looking for the slight increase that signified ovulation. To confirm, we used ovulation predictor tests. The process became a well-oiled machine. A sperm deposit in a sterile plastic cup was wrapped in aluminum foil and a towel to keep it warm. We protected the sample as we would a child on a cold winter day. The lab would then spin the sperm in a machine, separating the strongest ones for insemination. When it was my turn, I discretely left work for my appointment. Lying on the cold metal exam table, I was "turkey basted" and told to lie still for 10 minutes. I worried that 10 minutes couldn't possibly be enough time and that gravity would take over, causing the sperm to dribble out. I counted the ceiling tiles and willed the sperm to swim upstream to my fallopian tubes to meet my ready egg. I visualized the egg admitting one tiny sperm then re-sealing itself.

Sex became regulated through a strict schedule, and it wasn't romantic or fun. It had a single purpose: procreation. We were emotionally and physically spent. The crushing disappointment we felt each time I got my period stayed with us for days. It was hard to stay positive in the face of monthly failure. To make matters worse, we were continually barraged with very personal questions about our childless existence. "When are you going to have children?" "What are you waiting for; you're not getting any younger." These intrusive questions cut deep and infuriated us. My canned response became, "We'll tell you when there's something to know."

Pregnancy was omnipresent. Neighbors, colleagues, friends, and strangers were pregnant the "normal" way, which exacerbated my feelings of despair and yearning. While I could intellectually separate enough to express happiness for others, it broke my spirit. I felt sorry for myself and could think of nothing else. We had endured eight rounds of unsuccessful artificial insemination. Almost another year had passed. Perhaps this wasn't meant to be.

After a detailed conversation with our doctor, we were informed that artificial insemination had only a 10-15% success rate. We could continue this path and never conceive. We'd wasted time pursuing something with a statistically small chance of success, and I was angry. Angry with my doctor for leading us down a fruitless path, and angry with myself for not being a stronger, more well informed advocate. Some mother-to-be I was.

After discussing various options, we decided to pursue the most aggressive: in vitro fertilization. I mentally prepared to become a pincushion for syringes of hormones and drugs and endure two surgeries in the span of one month.

The world was preparing for Y2K and the imagined disasters that would befall. I too was focused on my own potential Armageddon. This was it. If the IVF didn't work, we would have to accept failure.

On December 31, 1999, I closed my eyes and remembered the biblical line, "Be fruitful and multiply." That was my desperate New Year's Eve wish and all that mattered to me.

Let the IVF work and I will do…anything.

We ordered the fertility drugs from a specialty pharmacy and practiced administering shots in an orange. Each morning I injected my stomach with one drug, and each night my husband gave me another shot in the deep muscle of the buttocks or thigh. My backside had a palette of bruises ranging from angry purple to faded yellow. I was a vessel for hormones that were trying to coax my body to produce eggs for harvest. I felt battered and inhuman.

As I laid in the recovery room after the egg retrieval, fuzzy from anesthesia, I knew something was wrong. I felt a heavy weight on my chest and couldn't breathe. The doctor told me I was "hyper-stimulated" from all of the drugs. My body had gone into a manic production mode and produced 23 eggs in a single ovulation cycle.

Because of my hyper-stimulation, I was placed on bed rest for one month. I had no strength and could draw only shallow breaths. I took a medical leave of absence from my job and spent my days watching re-runs of *The Nanny* and *Dallas*.

I felt like shit.

My 23 eggs were sorted and graded like a class of students. Those that had multiple cells were "A students," voted most likely to be fertilized. Others were average students with questionable potential, and some were dropouts. Of the A's, some were allowed to mingle with sperm naturally, and some were injected with sperm in a forced fertilization process.

On the transfer day, the doctor implanted me with three "A" fertilized eggs and casually remarked that if all three took, they could "select" one for termination. I couldn't even process what that meant at the time, and hoped never to have to make that decision.

After a few weeks, I returned to the doctor for blood work and a sonogram. Because my hormone levels were abnormally high from the hyper-stimulation, we couldn't rely on a traditional pregnancy test.

We were like swimmers lost at sea, caught between the panic of submersion and the hopefulness of rescue. Lying on yet another exam table, I waited with my arms tensed and fingernails digging into my palms. The blurry black and white images of the sonogram floated in waves, then sharpened. It looked like vast nothingness.

The doctor pointed to the screen and introduced us to A and B. Two embryos had taken. Two tiny beans. Before grasping the enormity of the news, I thought about the one who didn't make it. Was it a son or daughter? We would never know. We were relieved that we wouldn't be in the impossible position to "select" an embryo.

While I was thrilled to be pregnant, the irony of the situation was not lost on me. We were not in the room during the conception of our children. The implications were staggering. How could we be sure these were ours? Would we explain to them one day about their conception, and tell them they might encounter infertility as well—our unwitting genetic gift to them? I felt cheated of the experience of peeing on a stick and being the first to know a wonderful secret.

While there was joy, the instant worries of parenthood were thrust upon us. Were the babies healthy? Could I carry twins to term? Were there any genetic abnormalities that could have occurred in this science project, since we had the hubris to take the process out of nature's hands? Could we finally relax and enjoy this pregnancy, despite its high-risk status? It was hard to enjoy being pregnant when there was so much that could go wrong.

Despite our worries, the pregnancy was relatively normal. I gained over 70 pounds (at least five of which went to my feet) and carried an enormous belly. We played with name combinations memorializing our lost loved ones and prepared the nursery. The last month was spent on strict bed-rest trying to keep Baby A, whose head was positioned low and against my bladder, from making an early entrance.

At 36 weeks, I had a scheduled induction. There would be no water-breaking-scrambling-panicking for me. I'd packed my bag, installed the car seats, styled my hair, and shaved whatever I could reach. I expected everything to run smoothly according to plan. Only it didn't. As soon as the epidural needle pierced my skin, I became dizzy and couldn't breathe. Monitors beeped, and voices shouted as the room filled with at least 15 doctors and nurses. My orderly birth plan shattered. Unfortunately, my epidural had inadvertently become a full spinal block, and my body rebelled.

Metal instruments flashed and disappeared beneath the surgical sheet, and I pushed. Both boys were born within 12 minutes, each weighing 5½ pounds. They were healthy and beautiful, and I scanned them for differences to tell them apart.

As I lay in the recovery room, mentally and physically depleted, all I wanted was to hold our babies, but couldn't. No one realized that a misplaced epidural needle had paralyzed my legs. Over the next six weeks in rehabilitation I progressed from wheelchair to walker to cane. I was determined to recover because I had to. The babies needed their mom, and their needs motivated every step I relearned to take.

The road had been fraught with difficulty—from infertility to a high-risk pregnancy to a traumatic birth and recovery. But having our babies made all the difficulties fade into the background. Our babies' picture now hangs on the doctor's wall with all the other success stories.

Shanna Silva is an author, freelance writer, and two-time Tony-nominated Broadway producer. She writes for Kveller *and has a children's book set for publication in 2017. In between it all, she is raising three amazing and loud boys with her husband, Steven.*

TWO FOR ONE

BECKI MELCHIONE

"Wow, two for one! When did you find out that you were having twins?" A mom asked as we pushed our strollers along a shaded path, hoping that the continuous movement would soothe the sleeping infants.

"Early in the pregnancy," I replied because the whole story was more complicated than a brief conversation could ever convey. But even that answer was misleading.

My husband Luc and I knew that there was a chance of twins before we were pregnant. We created that possibility by transferring two embryos instead of one. The decision came after a tangled path of cancer and infertility during which we were forced to reevaluate every notion of motherhood we held. At that pivotal moment, when asked what we wanted to do, we looked at each other without question. "Two," we said simultaneously. "Let's transfer two embryos." Two increased our odds of having one baby. That's all we wanted.

Months of research and conversations around cancer and fertility produced no black and white choices, only the murkiness of unenviable statistics. Every step led to a compromise between hope and fear. The type of cancer I had, a melanoma of the eye, was albino rare. The majority of those diagnosed with it were members of AARP, not the PTA. Survival rates were projected over 20 years, a steady decline into the single digits. In 20 years, I would be 54.

Certain melanomas were known to be estrogen sensitive. That gave my oncologist pause. Dr. Pink had treated a woman in her early 30s, like me, whose melanoma spread in a hormone-fueled frenzy during her pregnancy. Dr. Pink's naturally relaxed demeanor turned grave. It was clear that her patient's outcome had not been good, but I couldn't ask what happened. Cancer casualty stories still spun me into a downward spiral of anxiety and worry.

"If you need someone to carry a baby for you, I'd be honored," my sister Cara had offered shortly after I began treatment. Her offer, previously stashed in the back of my mind, reemerged when Dr. Pink suggested that an alternative way to create our family would be safest.

Still, the idea of having a baby the usual way tumbled around the stubborn edges of my mind. I could do it, ignore my trusted doctor's advice, but it was an unknowable risk. Some days, I had come to terms with this. If I knew that she would have people to love her, my husband and our families, to raise her, I gladly would have given my life to bring the daughter I always imagined into the world. This way makes the world what I always imagined. It would have been one last way to say, "Screw cancer!"

Other days, I couldn't decide if it was fair to her to bring her into the world knowing that there was a significant chance of leaving her motherless. What damage would that do to a child, a teenager, a young woman? When you want something so desperately, you suddenly notice it everywhere. Soon, stories of women who grew up motherless appeared—in magazines, as a writing assignment from a fellow student, in conversations with a co-worker. Despite my fears that my daughter would be damaged forever, the universe presented the opposite. It said that she would survive and might even be stronger as a result.

But what struck me most were the memories these children of lost mothers held close: those of cooking together, decorating for holidays, perusing vacation photo albums, reading a favorite book, hugs after a tough day. "Mom" was a loving presence, not simply the woman who birthed them. That's what I wanted: to kiss her boo-boos and lay next to her reading stories that would waft her off to dreamland. I wanted to brush her hair into ponytails and braids and put funny makeup on her for Halloween. I wanted all those moments for my memories because, to her, they would be what Mom does. She wouldn't know how close she came to not having them, that they might have been Daddy kissing her hurts and Grammy braiding her hair. Having a surrogate was a gift, insurance on some level that I would be there for her.

To explore the surrogacy option, Luc and I saw a fertility specialist who confirmed that our plan was possible, just not in New York where we lived. Surrogacy in New York was illegal. We would have to go to a clinic in New Jersey or Pennsylvania to start the process. First, though, we needed to rule out any fertility issues on our end. Luc was thrilled that his little guys echoed his drive to success. They were in the top percentiles of volume, count, mobility and morphology. I couldn't say the same for myself. My ovaries had exhausted their store of eggs earlier than most women, and those that remained were like the bruised and broken fruit at the bottom of a basket. But still, if I couldn't bring her into the world myself, I craved that my genetic code be imprinted in her blood, for her to carry on a small part of me.

I was comfortable with the idea of Cara carrying my baby because she was of the same flesh, ate healthier than me, and had breezed through her two uneventful pregnancies with a calm peace that I admired. After we spoke with surrogacy lawyers, health insurance representatives, and fertility clinics, and just as we were about to start the process, my brother-in-law began to spiral apart, taking his marriage and my sister's offer with him. Suddenly, she needed to find a job to support her two young children because he shuffled in and out of hospitals and couldn't work. "I just can't do it right now. There's just so much stress, and I have no idea what's going to happen," she apologized again and again. I couldn't blame her, but I also couldn't wait anymore.

The first time we spoke with Heather was during a phone interview that the surrogacy agency set up. She laughed easily. Her humor and compassion shone when asked why she wanted to become a gestational carrier. We liked her immediately. She had three children of her own and didn't want to add another, but said, "I'm just one of those people who love being pregnant." It was her superpower. After seeing a good friend struggle with infertility, she thought, why not use her superpower to help someone else?

Five months later, Heather's and my menstrual cycles were coordinated for a round of in vitro fertilization. For two weeks I pumped myself full of hormones and hope. Although she was fertile soil, my ovaries failed, producing one flawed egg. It didn't nestle into her. Two weeks later, the pregnancy test came back negative. I was devastated.

We knew there was only one other option. It had been a part of the assisted fertility conversation whenever we spoke of using a surrogate and especially after my ovaries were declared nearly empty. Doctors and nurses routinely asked, "Will you be using your eggs or a donor's?" We always said "ours." But now, we had to consider donor eggs. With all of the costs approaching that of a college education, we couldn't afford another IVF cycle that most likely wouldn't work. Wrung out by all of the waiting and failing, my patience was thin. We exhausted every option. I just wanted to have a baby. Whether it was genetically related or not didn't matter anymore. We needed an egg donor who could provide lots of eggs, so even if our next transfer with Heather failed, we could try again and again if necessary.

I scoured hundreds of donor profiles looking for someone Luc would think was me if he saw her across a room. While I searched for similar heritage, appearance, intellect, and interests, Luc reviewed medical histories for genetic disease. Eventually, we settled on an anonymous woman in her early twenties, who had dark hair and eyes and a creative streak like me. She gave us 19 eggs. With Luc's sperm, our fertility team created enough blastocysts to select the strongest ones, those with a flourishing inner mass of cells and a well-formed outer layer.

The doctor showed us a chart with alternating gray and white columns with numbers in black. In one column, the age range of the egg donor, in the next, the number of eggs transferred, followed by the percent of pregnancies and live births. If any numbers could convey hope, these could.

"What's this column?" I asked, following the line for the 20 to 25-year-old donors, fresh embryos, with a gestational carrier, moving my eyes from the high numbers, 56% to 65%, to a gray column where the numbers dropped to less than 25%.

"That is the percent of multiple births. The more embryos you transfer," he traced a line under the row for one embryo versus two, "the more likely you are to become pregnant." His finger lingered under a particularly high number—65%. "But you're also more likely to have a multiple birth," his finger moved to the next column. My eyes fixated on the highest percentage, that 65%. If we transferred two fresh embryos, our chances of conceiving were better than choosing black or red on a roulette table. The statistic in that last column hardly mattered. I glanced and promptly forgot about it.

Moments before the transfer, a nurse handed me an image taken through a microscope of two grainy bubbles, hardly more than a few dozen cells. The two weeks between the transfer and our first pregnancy test, Luc and I packed up everything we owned and moved from New York to Baltimore for Luc's new job. Packing and unpacking boxes, carefully wrapping papers and bubble wrap over our wedding china and Luc's grandmother's crystal cocktail glasses kept me focused and too busy to obsess about what might be. Luc's first day in his new position was the same date as our pregnancy test.

The X-Files theme burst from my phone. Sharon, the nurse who Heather and I spoke with daily for Heather's monitoring, said, "Hello, Becki?" Then, her calm demeanor felt reassuring; now it seemed less so.

"Heather had her test this morning." She's too calm, I thought, we've failed again. Disappointment began to creep in.

She continued. "It's positive. You're pregnant." For a quick moment, all my worry evaporated.

"Oh, my, God!" My eyes brightened, but immediately she hedged.

"This is just the first test. Let's see how it goes in the next few weeks."

I texted Luc our sign: +

I called Heather. "Did you hear from Nurse Sharon?"

"Yes! It's so exciting."

"Ok, I'm going to try not to call you all of the time and annoy you from now on. But I don't know if that's going to be possible."

"Don't worry. Call me as much as you want," she reassured me.

Just as Heather and our egg donor had been closely monitored through the IVF cycle, the early weeks of our pregnancy commanded more tests. Every few days Heather's hormone levels were evaluated, and Nurse Sharon called with the results. The first beta level was 209; for our first failed transfer, it was 50. A good sign. The next test was three days later. The beta tripled, another good sign. Too good of a sign. Luc did a quick Google search.

"There's a significant possibility that there is more than one. According to this chart, 764 is high for a three-day beta and indicates the probability of two embryos," he announced in his physician's voice.

Two weeks later, Heather called me from the ultrasound chair. "There are two! Two sacs!"

"What? Really? Oh my God!?" I laughed so hard that Heather started laughing too.

"Wouldn't it be so fun if I got to carry twins?" Heather had said multiple times. Now she gushed, "I'm so excited! I can't believe I'm carrying twins!"

"Oh my God, oh my God! There are two sacs—TWO! Twins!" I screeched into the phone to Luc next.

"What are we going to do?"

A twin pregnancy could be so much more complicated. Don't twins usually deliver about four weeks early? Will Heather have to be on bed rest? For how long? What do we have to cover if she's on bed rest? Childcare? Transportation? Cleaning? Can we afford that? Isn't there a higher risk for gestational diabetes? Would Heather's health be at risk? From zero to two in nine months, but not just two babies, double of everything: two cribs, two high chairs, two swings, four car seats, 10 sets of pajamas, 20 onesies, 40 sets of bottles. As the numbers multiplied, any sense of possibility that we could make this work sunk into a deep pool of uncertainty. How would it all fit in our apartment? Would we ever sleep? How would we feed, soothe, bathe, clothe two infants?

Luc was calm, as he tended to be in the face of emergencies. Or maybe because he wasn't going to be the one home with two infants 24 hours a day, seven days a week.

"One baby would be a lot of work, two will be a lot of work, but we won't know any different," he said.

Had I been the one pregnant, I would have felt my breasts ache, my stomach turn, my sense of smell heighten. Feeling the changes to my body would have added to the anticipation and excitement. Because it wasn't my body, the babies did not influence every thought and decision I made from what to eat, what to drink, what to do. Partially, it was a coping mechanism. Our pregnancy felt tenuous. One of the sacs could be absorbed by the other, our fertility specialist said, and we would have one baby. Or there was the possibility that both would disappear. Most women wouldn't even know they were pregnant yet. The human body is still a mystery. Despite everything we think we know, all we can do is try to assist natural processes and hope for the best.

Still, we were closer to having our family than ever before and every time I thought of those two sacs, I couldn't help but dream of who they would become.

A few days later, I decided that I couldn't not do anything. We had waited too long, tried too hard, and spent too much to get to this point. I was in—all in. If I had anything to do with it, by sheer force of hope, I was going to bring our babies into the world. My only way was to take care of Heather. So I bought her the things that I would have bought if I were pregnant. A BPA-free water bottle, saltines, chocolate, peppermint tea, antacid, folic acid, multivitamins, healthy snack bars, and I packed them all into a big cardboard box with little notes like 'Yay for chocolate!' or 'For when you're starving between breakfast #1 and breakfast #2' on each of them. Heather was nauseous, tired, emotional, achy and sore. The least I could do was to try to make her more comfortable.

"It's weird to say that I'm glad that you're not feeling well, but it's a good sign," I told Heather over and over, every time she called or texted with a new symptom.

From the obstetrician's office for her 12-week ultrasound, Heather called, said a brief hello and then put the phone toward the thumping amplified by computer speakers.

"Can you hear it? There's baby A!" She chirped. Then a pause, and again the thumping. "And that's baby B!"

Hearing their heartbeats made them more real, three-dimensional. All at once they weren't embryos anymore, but babies—my babies. I took a deep breath and as I exhaled, a certainty set in. This ultrasound marked the end of the first trimester, the end of the high risk of losing one or both of them. Although we'd tried to be confident that this whole process would work, the truth was my optimism was hedged by Luc's caution. But now, it was almost certain that we would have twins.

As they grew and began to twist and turn and kick, Heather joked, "These girls are really active! I definitely have the easy part. Once they're born, they're all yours!"

And they were all ours. At 38 weeks, Heather delivered my two little miracles. At their naming ceremony, we introduced my daughters to 19 members of their extended family, grandparents, aunts, uncles and cousins. "Look at that, two for one!" My uncle Rocky bellowed upon seeing them.

"You don't know how lucky you are!"

I do.

Becki Melchione's writing about young adult cancer, infertility and raising twins has appeared in Brain, Child; Literary Mama; Cargo Literary *and* Kaleidoscope Magazine. *She's been working on a memoir about choosing hope through cancer and infertility for too long to admit. Her current home is in the Philadelphia suburbs with her husband, the girls (twin daughters) and the boys (two cats).*

JOURNAL IT

Write your thoughts and feelings down. Capture the moments. Life with multiples is exciting and busy, and it's easy to forget the little things and details. Here is a writing prompt to help you along.

Infertility is an emotional rollercoaster. Write down the things that you have learned from your struggles with infertility.

PREGNANCY

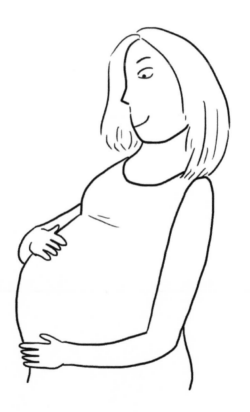

PREGNANCY

BEST PRACTICES FOR A HEALTHY MULTIPLES PREGNANCY

―――――――――――――――――――――――――――――――――――――

ALISON LEE

Twins occur naturally in about one in 250 pregnancies, triplets in about one in 10,000 pregnancies, and quadruplets in about one in 700,000 pregnancies. The main factor that increases your chances of having a multiple pregnancy is the use of infertility treatment, but, of course, there are also genetic factors.

All of the healthy practices in a singleton pregnancy still apply in a multiples gestation. However, there are several things you should do to stay healthy and happy during your multiples pregnancy.

- Carrying more than one baby requires special dietary needs. Consider making healthy protein shakes several times a day to stay nourished. You'll probably not be able to eat large meals, so grazing throughout the day is key. Keep packets of nuts or other protein-packed sources around your house and in your car at all times.

- Do not be alarmed by the term "high-risk," especially if you're pregnant with twins. Yes, there are more risks with carrying more than one baby, but it depends on many factors—your age, overall health, previous childbirth history, genetics, and lifestyle. The major issues to consider are preterm labor, bed rest and Caesarean sections, so talk to your doctor. Do take

53

precautions because a multiple pregnancy is a strain on your body.

- Rest, rest, rest. Pregnancy is tiring, and even more so with multiples. Implement a daily rest period and lie down for 20 to 30 minutes, especially when you've entered the second trimester. Do not do too much, and take modified bed rest after 20 weeks, even if it isn't doctor-mandated.

- Put a support system in place. When you're on bed rest, there isn't much you can do. When friends and family offer meal deliveries, help with household chores or carpooling (if you have older kids), say yes!

- Be prepared for more doctor appointments than usual. Multiples pregnancies are monitored closely, as your doctor will want to make sure that you're staying healthy and the babies are growing well. Here's where your support system will prove essential.

A multiples pregnancy is challenging, but it's also amazing and an experience like no other. Embrace it, and stay positive. Congratulations!

I'LL TAKE THREE

KIRSTEN GANT

Do you ever have friends or family staying with you and you find you spend 97% of your time loading, running and emptying your dishwasher? Then you sit down, just to gulp down a cup of coffee in the three minutes you've reserved for such activities and you unwittingly glance at the sink, only to discover it is once again piled high with dirty dishes and an angry mess of cutlery? Though you may wear your hostess smile like a badge of courage, you're inwardly screaming, "I'm sick of loading this stupid dishwasher! When is this house load of people leaving already?"

Welcome to my world, my friends. Only our house load of folks arrived all at once. And they are not going anywhere.

Once upon a time we were a quiet family. Some may say even tranquil. We lived in our calm house with our calm child, who can best be described as a "fooler baby." A fooler baby patiently waits to be given their bottle, and smiles sweetly through the foulest of diaper changes. In short, a fooler baby fools you into wanting additional babies. It is when those additional babies arrive—screaming bloody murder at unknown causes at all hours of the night—that you realize you have indeed been duped by your firstborn child.

Entranced by my fooler baby, I wanted another child something fierce. I worried incessantly that my oldest would be an only child. Doctors informed me that I was a lazy ovulator ("C'mon ovaries; stop being such a pair of sloths!") and that I would need to go on a drug to help stimulate those lazy clowns. They assured me that I would be closely monitored to ensure I didn't produce too many eggs at once.

So I popped a few pills a few times a month and went on my merry way, dreaming of chubby baby cheeks and tiny dimpled hands. Two months later I was elated to learn I was pregnant, "Score one for my lazy ovaries!" and couldn't wait to get to my OB-GYN for my first ultrasound. My husband had several meetings that day, so I told him not to sweat it. I'd head to the ultrasound on my own and call him after. I smiled as the ultrasound tech chatted incessantly about the rain until she stopped talking and said, "Oh my." She called for her supervisor, who checked the monitor and said gleefully, "Oh Lordy! Ma'am, we see three heartbeats."

I was silent, until I calmly asked, "So the baby has three hearts?"

"No honey. Looks like you're having triplets."

"Oh." Clearly I am not so quick on the uptake. "I think I need to talk to the doctor." The now flustered ultrasound technician tracked down my poor OB-GYN on the golf course and explained my situation.

"Sit tight, Kirsten," he assured me. "We'll do a follow-up ultrasound next week to rule out a phantom baby. This doesn't seem right. I mean…wow."

I stumbled out of the office half an hour later, images of three hearts and phantom babies floating in my head. I looked down at my trembling hand to see my phone was ringing. It was my husband. In the words of my toddler, "I feel uh-oh."

"How was it? Everything okay?" my husband asked excitedly.

I took a deep breath. Blurting out, "We're having triplets!" over the phone seemed downright wrong. Instead I managed to say calmly, "Everything was great, honey. I'll see you at home." I intended to drive straight home, but my car seemed to steer itself to my sister's house instead. Aside from my husband, she was the only other person who knew I was pregnant. I stood on her doorstep holding out my ultrasound images with a trembling hand. She looked at the three little blobs on the ultrasound, then up at me. I burst into tears. She led me in and sat me down. "Okay," she said, patting my back while I bawled, "You can cry about this once, and only once. After that, you need to get excited. This is happening. You're having three babies." I knew she was right. In my gut, I knew there was no phantom baby, no incorrect ultrasound. I was having three babies, my babies.

Just like that I stopped blubbering and started giggling at the absurdity of it all. I wiped the tears from my cheeks and headed home. My husband came bounding down the stairs when he saw me, holding our sweet little boy in his arms. "Let me see! Let me see!" he demanded, holding out a hand for the ultrasound picture.

"Well, I'm very glad I married you," I began, handing him the picture. "Because we are having triplets." He looked from me to the picture, the picture to me, and then sat down on the stairs. Our toddler jumped from his arms and began to run around in circles, and still my husband was silent. He placed his head in his hands. I started to panic. After a torturous eternity (or possibly 40 seconds) he looked up. "Well okay," he said, "let's have triplets."

In that moment the hazy news of triplets became a reality. We were having three babies, and even though they were just lima bean-sized at time, we loved that trio. Our trio. We loved them when we were advised (and declined the advice) that selective reduction of one of more babies would likely ensure the survival of the others. We loved them when we were told some or all might have Down syndrome. We loved them when strangers would ask me if I was trying to be like the Octomom (Um, seriously?).

Carrying triplets tested my will, my faith and my spine. Still we fought on, through worry, health scares, and nights filled with "what ifs". At 36½ weeks, our triad arrived, a trio of skinny, screaming aliens here to invade our lives with midnight feedings and endless diaper changes. They were loud and demanding. They were our miracles.

Now at a very active six years old, our house often resembles the scene in *Gremlins*. You know, the one where the monsters have taken control and are gleefully swinging from the chandeliers. I have given up trying to keep a tidy house and now settle for a mildly-controlled, pleasant mess of a home. Sure, there is usually unidentified sticky goo on the bottom of my shoe, but if I can still find the remote control and my car keys, it's a good day.

At this stage, we still get our fair share of comments in public, my four munchkins and I. "Are you running a day camp?" is a popular one. So is "My, you sure have your hands full!" But my favorite comment is, "Better you than me!" I always smile inwardly at that one. In fact, I agree with them. I also think it's better me than them. In this life, we all get a few miracles. Mine just came wrapped in three baby blankets and screaming with gusto. And I wouldn't trade them for all the quiet and calmness in the world.

Kirsten Gant is a freelance writer, Barre fitness instructor, and mother of 6-year-old triplets and a 9-year-old big brother living in Marietta, GA. Kirsten's first children's book, The Matter of the Moo Cow, *was published last spring and is available on Etsy and in many local shops and bookstores. Kirsten hopes to have her next children's book,* The Matter of the May Mouse, *on sale next spring.*

NEWS OF THE CENTURY

ALLIE CAPO-BURDICK

There are many moments in my life I will never forget; the moment my dad told me my mother had died, marrying my husband on a beach in Key West, running the Boston marathon and, perhaps most life-changing, my first ultrasound after I found out I was pregnant.

The memory of that doctor visit now is like a dream. It flashes and pauses, stops and starts. I hear only my heartbeat, and the rest of the room has gone silent. There's something I'm holding. Is it a picture? It's a fuzzy black and white image. I know it's important, but I can't think straight. I need to focus. I need to remember what brought me here.

It was the day of my first official doctor's appointment, and I was giddy with excitement.

I was eight weeks into my pregnancy and still getting used to the idea. I'm the epitome of a Type A personality. I'm a planner, a doer with a capital D. I research everything and follow through with every project I start, so you can imagine the list of questions I had for that first appointment. I've been known to be a tad over-prepared, but I'm also very organized—which would become an invaluable asset nine months later.

Now, if you've ever been pregnant, then you know that first doctor appointment is more like an interrogation of questions about the family health history of you and your husband. Be prepared to know everything about his family's health, including what his grandfather's blood pressure was. After the family health history assault, you're "rewarded" with all kinds of samples and information in cutesy little bags; all of which are sponsored by some baby formula company, and everyone is buzzing around you like you're a goddess. Okay, maybe not exactly like a goddess, but it's a pretty ridiculous little circus at that first appointment. My head was spinning before I even saw a doctor.

All this should have been a giant heads-up to me about the things that were to come, but I was blissfully unaware. These were also the last moments before my bubble burst like so much fluid in some gross sac of amniotic fluid that pops one day and ends up all over your kitchen floor.

But, I digress.

My doctor finally appeared in my waiting room, and I thought she was perfect. She was a runner! She had four kids! This was all going exactly as I had planned. We chatted happily about all the wonderful things pregnancy brings, and she was so happy to see I was already in great shape and yes, why not continue doing all the things I was already doing like running and biking until I felt uncomfortable?

Then, almost as an afterthought, she suggested we do an ultrasound since they had one in the office. My first thought was YES! How cool! I get to do this on the first visit? Yay me. So I waited a moment as instructed, then was ushered into the little ultrasound room with the big computer, the little monitor, and a slightly intimating woman holding what can be a very intimidating object *(the transducer, which allows the doctor to see the baby)* that closely resembles a huge vibrator.

So there I lay, like so many women before me, with legs propped up in stirrups, waiting for a glimpse at a tiny little bean that would grow into the love of my life.

What happens next is a blur, but it went something like this:

Tech: Let's see if we can get a look at him *(slight pause)* or BOTH of them!

Me (glancing at the screen and seeing TWO little black dots and thinking to myself 'WHAT THE HELL?' but saying…): Wait what? What are you talking about?

It was as if she suddenly stopped speaking English, but yes, there *they* were, plain as day, and I got my first glimpse of those two little babies.

Holy shit.

The first thing I thought, for the first time in my life was I.Can.Not.Do.This.

This is not a phrase I am accustomed to. Remember I am a Type A woman and an athlete. I survived my mother dying when I was a teenager; I have run seven marathons as an adult and began running my own fitness business. I can do anything. I am woman, hear me roar and all that bullshit. But here I was looking at two little black dots on a monitor and thinking, "I can't do this."

What I was thinking must have been all over my face, and registered with the ultrasound technician because, before I knew it, she was handing me a box of tissues. Was I crying? No! I was freaking out so why was she handing me tissues? How about a Valium and some tequila?

After an awkward pause she said, "I'll get Dr. Whatshername because she'll probably want to talk to you again." No kidding.

The ultrasound technician gave me some pictures of my two little beans and sent me out into the waiting room. This would be the first of many times in the years since that I would feel like a sedated mental patient. I took a seat and stared at those pictures. I think I may have been drooling.

The other women in the waiting room began to notice and were looking at me with concern. When I told them that I just discovered I was pregnant with twins, they erupted into laughter. Oh yes, they loved it. They thought it was the best thing ever that I had been surprised with this news and that I was completely freaking out. Laugh it up, people! It's not you—it's me! I could picture them going home later that night and telling their significant others all about the adorable lunatic in the doctor's office who just found out she was having twins.

If I had been paying attention, I would have had my first realization of how much happiness twins bring, even to strangers. The immense joy at the announcement of the twins' impending birth was astounding. The thousands of smiles and outpouring of love we received after they were born was beautiful.

But, that day, I still had so much more to process.

Eventually my gynecologist, who I love as much as any woman can love an OB-GYN, came to my rescue. This wasn't the first time. The first time my beloved Dr. K saw me was when I was 17 after my mom died of ovarian cancer. I was scared on so many levels. Dr. K sat me down in her office and with her steel blue eyes looked right at me and said, "So, tell me what's going on. I hear you've been through a lot." And she *meant* it. I mean she *really* meant it.

As luck would have it Dr. K was in the office the day I got the shock of my life and came out into the waiting room.

Dr. K: "What's going on? All the nurse told me was to see you."

Me: (totally panicked): "Oh my God—I'm pregnant with twins!"

Dr. K: "That is fantastic! You're perfect for it." And she gave me the first of what would be so many amazing congratulatory hugs.

Then she took me into her office and gave me some water and, just like she always did, she talked me through it and told me it was going to be okay. She offered to call someone to drive me home (this is how hysterical I was!) and then walked me down to my car.

Once I got to my car I realized I still couldn't drive so I called the only person it was reasonable to call in such a situation—my sister-in-law Melissa. She was six months pregnant at the time and knew I was at the doctor that day.

Melissa: "Hi—how did it go?"

Me: "Holy sweet mother of God I am freaking out—it's twins! Twins!"

Her (laughing): "Oh my God shut up! Are you serious? Oh my God. Okay. Okay. It's going to be okay."

Me: "It's going to be okay? Did you hear what I said?"

Melissa (still laughing a little more hysterically at me): "It's okay. You have to calm down. It's going to be fine. This is perfect."

Me: "Perfect for who?"

Before she hung up, she asked if she could tell my brother or did I want to, and I told her to go ahead and tell him. She hung up the phone and texted my brother: "I have the news of the century."

It was definitely the news of the century. No one knew I was pregnant, or even trying to have a baby, so the shock factor was off the charts. Once I told my husband, telling the rest of the family was some of the most fun I have ever had.

As it turns out, like most husbands, mine was not where he was supposed to be that afternoon. He had decided to meet his mom at a doctor's appointment and called to tell me he was leaving as I was driving home. Once I heard his voice it was all over. He guessed the news. He was joking of course, saying, "Don't tell me it's twins?" Ha ha ha. Well, the joke was on him. He had to pull the car over and take it all in. Needless to say, we didn't get much sleep for the next few months.

Telling my friends and relatives was equally exciting. Many people announce pregnancies, but announcing you're pregnant with twins is something special because people do not know what to say or do in the very best way.

Telling my dad and my aunt was the best. My aunt started scream-crying on the phone, and her coworkers thought there was something wrong. No, we're Italian, and a good mozzarella is exciting so you can imagine what the news of twins did to her.

I had to call my dad out of a meeting while he was at work. He thought I was going to tell him I wasn't pregnant! Nope—just the opposite. In the years since, his grandsons have been the greatest joy in his life. He even loves me more for bringing his two best buddies into the world.

The calls went on and on. Most just couldn't believe that this tiny Cuban/Italian girl, who much preferred running to children, was not only having one baby, but two.

Announcing my pregnancy was only the tip of the overwhelming happiness iceberg. My boys have brought immeasurable joy, just by the identical sight of them.

As the years have passed, I realized that not only could I do this twin thing; I cannot imagine doing anything else.

Allie Capo-Burdick is happiest when writing or sweating. Her work has appeared in Runner's World, Women's Running Magazine, USA Trialathon Magazine *and countless other health and fitness publications. Allie is also a competitive athlete on the Oiselle Volée team and has represented Team USA in a duathlon competition. When not updating her blog* VITA—Train for Life, *she is busy with her twin boys and husband, living a big life in the Northeast.*

EXTREME PREGNANCY

EILEEN C. MANION

"Did you take any drugs?"

Advil for a headache? Antihistamine for hay fever? Who remembers these things?

The young, dark-haired technician seemed hostile. Or was I imagining that? She was looking at the monitor, not at me, while I gazed intently at her pale, freckled face, trying to read the expression in her brown eyes. Her forehead puckered, her head moved as if she were counting something on the screen.

The evening before I'd read an article about a young woman in Seattle who'd been arrested and charged by an overzealous prosecutor for fetal abuse because she'd smoked a joint while she was pregnant and her baby had been born brain-damaged. Could they put me in jail for taking a Claritin? Best to deny everything.

"No," I answered sharply, indignantly, trying to sound like a respectable, upstanding citizen.

"Are you ready for a shock?"

Vaguely remembering a Margaret Atwood short story I'd recently read, I'd been joking about finding a hairball in my uterus while I was driving to the Queen Elizabeth Hospital in Charlottetown. Only two weeks earlier, a family doctor in Montague had come up with positive results on a pregnancy test. That was shock enough. I didn't want another one.

A late period was hardly unusual for me, but the sudden weight gain and terminal fatigue I'd started experiencing during this 1987 Prince Edward Island vacation seemed odd. Premature menopause? Uterine tumor? I peed in a cup and dipped in a pregnancy test stick. Negative. Must be cancer; so I went to the doctor expecting a death sentence.

The doctor had the unflappable air of a young man who'd already dealt with many neurotic women; he wouldn't refer me to an oncologist before checking for a more routine explanation for my symptoms.

Twelve weeks seemed early for my first ultrasound, but in the doctor's rural practice where most women my age were taking care of grandchildren, he probably hadn't seen many women coming in pregnant for the first time at 40.

Despite my brave attempts at gallows humor on the way to the hospital, I was not prepared for a shock. With my blue stretch pants and cotton underwear pulled down and bunched around my ankles, I felt vulnerable, undignified, and resentful of the young technician whose mother was probably about my age.

"No," I repeated as emphatically as before. "Tell me what you see."

"Triplets," she replied with an air of triumph, as if she'd succeeded in playing a clever sales trick on an unsuspecting customer.

"That's impossible."

Having triplets was something I might have read about in a women's magazine while waiting in line at the grocery store. Not something that had ever happened to anyone I knew. No. Multiples don't run in my family. Nor my partner's.

The technician turned the monitor around so I could see the screen. With her index finger, she pointed to what she claimed were three fetal heartbeats. I remained unconvinced.

"I'll get a doctor." Maybe she was annoyed that I didn't believe her.

She returned in a few minutes with a thin, elderly gentleman in a white coat. The two of them gazed intently at the screen.

"Those are the first triplets we've had since we got this new equipment." The doctor looked impressed. Both of them seemed so pleased with the achievement of their state-of-the-art machine that they'd forgotten all about me.

"Can I survive this pregnancy?" I asked.

"Oh, don't worry. You're healthy. You'll be fine."

To me, he sounded very cavalier: what did he know about my health? He'd barely glanced at me in his intent pleasure with the hospital's new technology.

"We haven't had many triplets on the Island. Only two sets that I remember." The doctor was still chatting with the ultrasound technician, leaving me to climb off the table and pull up my pants.

That question about drugs—she'd meant fertility, not recreational. No. I hadn't taken those either. I was so convinced that I'd been rendered infertile by scarring from a bad case of pelvic inflammatory disease in the early 1970s that I'd stopped worrying about birth control several years earlier.

All that was running through my mind as I staggered out of the hospital to tell my partner, Norman, the news.

"You're going to think I'm joking, but I'm not."

Since neither of us knew anything about multiples, we headed straight to Charlottetown's largest bookstore and bought the only volume they had on twins and triplets. Most of the book was about twins; all sorts of studies had been done on twins, but triplets? Not much. It occurred to me that there just hadn't yet been enough of them for psychologists and other researchers to study. Twins often appear in myth, fiction, and fable, but triplets?

After I'd read enough about the risks of a triplet pregnancy and premature birth, I surmised that before the existence of modern NICUs, not many triplets survived to make it into myth or fiction or history. Unless you count the Fates, or the Trinity—God as triplets?

When friends heard news of my extreme pregnancy, they were amused by the cosmic joke. I was probably the least kid-savvy person in my social circle. Whenever colleagues had children, I always offered to babysit to help out the new parents, but none ever asked me to do it more than once. I took this as a sign of my ineptitude. In truth, I was frightened of babies. They seemed fragile, unpredictable, and smelly. You couldn't discuss novels with them or even gossip, so my limited repertoire of social interaction was useless.

A few days after the traumatic ultrasound, while I was still trying to absorb the shock, I returned to the doctor, but he didn't want to talk to me.

"Go back to Montreal and get yourself a good obstetrician." A 40-year-old with a first pregnancy was bad enough, but one having triplets? That was way beyond his skill set.

So I cut short my vacation, drove back to Montreal, and started looking for "a good obstetrician." I called my family doctor; he said he'd call back with a referral, but he didn't. When I called the gynecologist who'd delivered the babies of one of my friends, she said the possible complications were out of her league, but she suggested I call Dr. Alice Benjamin.

Dr. Benjamin gave me an appointment within a week—I was just the sort of patient she enjoyed. Normal pregnancies were tedious for her; she felt her skills were wasted. What she enjoyed was the extreme pregnancy. She was an Indian woman about my age with a competent air and calming presence. I imagined she must start her days with several sun salutations and at least 30 minutes of meditation.

At our first meeting, and at many subsequent ones, she drew a picture of three water balloons to represent the three amniotic sacs.

"Gravity is your enemy," she repeated every time I saw her. Whenever I was standing, pressure was exerted on the cervix—like water trying to escape from the opening of a balloon. The solution? Remain prone.

From August to December, I remained at home, mostly lying down. Although the triplet pregnancy was confirmed with another ultrasound, I didn't believe that I'd ever end up with three babies; I remained convinced that something would go wrong, but I didn't want whatever that was to be my fault, so I obeyed doctor's orders.

Dr. Benjamin sent me off to a nutritionist who gave detailed instructions on what I should and should not eat. She recommended eating several snacks in addition to three regular meals: lots of protein, few carbs, lots of vegetables and fruit, a liter of milk a day. No alcohol. No more than one cup of coffee a day.

If I didn't eat before going to bed, I'd either wake up in the middle of the night feeling starved or get up in the morning with a soul-destroying headache. Eating for four is time-consuming. Planning meals and snacks took up a good portion of any given day.

I can count on one hand the number of times I left the house from August to December, aside from visits to the obstetrician. I did make two outings for new clothes: a couple pairs of men's sweat pants, size extra large and an enormous yellow terry cloth robe that made me look like a walking tent.

I heard about a sale of baby paraphernalia organized by the Montreal chapter of a twins' organization. I felt I should go and buy some of the stuff I might need. One of my friends agreed to drive me and give advice since she had two children and knew the drill. When we arrived at the church basement, I felt overwhelmed—what is all this stuff, what's it for, and how much do I need? I bought a pile of undershirts, at my friend's suggestion, and a few small blankets. I knew there must be more I should have, but had no idea what it was. However, many experienced parents eager to donate outgrown equipment to a good cause, offered me things:

two cribs, two car seats, several garbage bags full of blankets, pajamas, quilts, diapers. Toys. Books. Stuffed animals. My apartment started looking like a Goodwill drop-off area.

The bigger I got, the less energy I had, so lying around reading all the time didn't frustrate me the way I imagined it would. Whenever I got tired of reading, I had a few amusements unavailable to others: I could lie in the bathtub and feel several organisms swimming around inside my abdomen. It felt like a litter of puppies. Or I could lie on the carpet, turn on some music, and imagine that the three moving embryos were dancing to the beat.

Only during the last two weeks of the pregnancy did I begin to feel miserable. Once I tipped the scales at 170 pounds, I stopped weighing myself. Then I started retaining fluid, and my head felt like it contained one of those water balloons Dr. Benjamin kept drawing. The fluid retention led to an ear infection, for which she reluctantly prescribed antibiotics.

From the beginning, Dr. Benjamin warned that the babies would be premature and would have to be delivered by C-section. Her target was to bring the pregnancy to 34 weeks, just three shy of the normal term. So far, I'd lasted 31 weeks, and she was still hoping to keep going, but I was fed up with the compliant patient role and guiltily wanted the whole thing to be over.

Saturday, December 5th, I woke around six a.m. and noticed the bed was wet. My first thought was that, in addition to every other humiliation I'd suffered, I'd become incontinent. As I rushed to the bathroom, my brain switched on.

"My water broke. We better go to the hospital," I yelled.

Norman called a cab to take us to the Royal Victoria Hospital.

Aside from all the wetness, I didn't seem to be having anything else you see in movies of women giving birth—no labor pains, no contractions.

The intern on duty put me in a wheelchair and wheeled me into a small room with a bed long enough for a dwarf. Despite its inadequacy, I somehow hauled myself into it. The nurses positioned me on my left side and attached a fetal monitor to one of the babies. Then they wheeled in a second fetal monitor and attached it to another. Every half hour they'd come in to turn me over so they could make a switch and check on the third.

Soon an obstetrical resident came around to inspect this interesting case. He ordered a complicated intravenous cocktail: a drug that was supposed to prevent contractions and another that was supposed to jump-start fetal lung development. The trick was that the lung development drug was supposed to take 72 hours. I had to endure the ordeal that long to allow the cocktail to do its work.

"Where's Dr. Benjamin?" I desperately needed reassurance.

"I talked to her on the phone. She'll drop in this afternoon to see you."

When Dr. Benjamin arrived, I'd been licking ice cubes and been turned over so many times, I felt like I must be sufficiently chilled and grilled for her. However, she didn't remove her coat or hat; she stood several feet away from the bed, hovering in the doorway as if she thought what I had might be contagious.

"I don't want to disturb anything down there. The drug that's supposed to promote fetal lung development takes 72 hours, and besides, it's not a good idea to deliver on Sunday. Not enough staff. We'll do it Monday morning. Be patient."

I put on my most stoical smile as she turned to waltz down the corridor.

"I'll examine you tomorrow. See how you're doing," she called as she walked away to her shopping or concert or whatever she had planned for the day.

During the night that followed, I can't say that I felt lonely or neglected. Every half hour a nurse came in to flip me over and reposition the fetal monitors. The parade of medical students, interns, and residents who trooped through spent more time looking at the printouts than at me, but they were all friendly, courteous, optimistic. Everyone seemed to think the process was on track.

The drug mixture had a weird effect: I felt like I was on speed. My mind raced and I was convinced that if I'd had pen and paper available, I could have written a whole novel. By 4 a.m. I was exhausted, and my bladder had given up on me. When the resident ordered a catheter, I burst into tears.

The young, dark-haired nurse who came next to check on me looked vaguely familiar.

"Do you teach at Dawson College?" she asked.

I'd always been afraid that I'd run into a former student at some awkward moment.

I stopped sniffling long enough to establish that she'd taken a course with me that I'd called "Women in Canada and Quebec" a few years earlier. I pulled myself together to endure the rest of the night.

Sunday morning, Dr. Benjamin returned. This time, she did take off her coat and asked if I'd felt any contractions.

"No." Though I certainly wished that I had.

She smiled, pleased that we were holding steady and could make it through to Monday; nonetheless, she took a quick look at my cervix.

"You've started dilating. We'll have to do it today." At the beginning of the pregnancy, she had promised me an epidural so I could remain conscious during the birth, but now she said that would take too long, so I had to have general anesthesia. Only later did she tell me that I was already eight centimeters dilated, but she didn't want to admit it and panic the staff.

After being rushed off to the operating room, I don't remember anything until I woke in what someone told me was the afternoon, but I was in so much pain that all I wanted was to go back to sleep. I'd like to think that I asked the nurses about the status of the babies, but all I remember is insisting they give me more drugs. At some point, I took in the information that they were all alive—three girls.

Monday I woke to six inches of snow outside and four layers of fog in my head. I was too weak to descend two floors to neonatal intensive care, so two nurses brought the three babies into my room and let me view them for about 30 seconds. As babies, they weren't convincing, reminding me of a dream I'd once had in which I'd packed three doll-sized infants into a suitcase, then lost them in the airport.

Tuesday, one of the nurses insisted I get up and walk around, so, like a good mother should, I decided to check on the babies. In the elevator, the obstetrical resident asked cheerfully, "How's the litter?"

"I guess they're okay—that's what they tell me." One of the pediatric residents had reassured me, "They're the healthiest triplets we've ever seen." To me, they looked like concentration camp survivors. Each weighed about three pounds. For the first few days, I saw them encased in plastic boxes attached to tubes, wires, and monitors. I touched them by putting a finger into one of the little holes in the front of the box. Since the preemie room was brutally well lit, noisy with monitors beeping, staff hurrying here and there, all the infants had their eyes closed. They might as well still have been in the womb.

After a week, Dr. Benjamin liberated me, but the babies had to stay in the hospital until they gained three pounds, sucked formula from a bottle, and remembered to breathe. All of that would take at least six weeks—about the time they would have been born if they'd been full-term.

Norman and I went back every day for several hours. Once the girls were out of the plastic boxes, we could hold each of them for a little while. Did they take this opportunity to bond with their parents? Hard to say, since they seemed to sleep through the experience. Finally, on Christmas Day, I was able to feed one from a bottle. She woke long enough to drink half of it, and then fell asleep again

One Sunday morning, a few weeks after the birth, I woke at home with that, "What's going on? Where am I?" feeling.

Then reality jolted me for the first time—I have three daughters. How would I cope? Would I bring them home, get them mixed up, and forget to feed one of them? I felt as if I'd been promoted to a management position for which I wasn't qualified. However, I had no choice; I would have to learn on the job.

Eileen C. Manion grew up in New York and moved to Montreal in 1969 where she got her Ph.D. in English at McGill University. Since the mid-1970s, she has been teaching English at Dawson College in Montreal. In 1987, she had triplet daughters, one of whom currently lives in Canada, while the other two are in the U.S.

THE MAP OF A TRIPLET PREGNANCY

MEGAN WOOLSEY

Waddling like I was crippled by a 20-pound tumor protruding from my abdomen, I made my way slowly into the perinatologist's office. Being fashion-forward, I was wearing a tan knitted beanie that stretched over my ears, which I later regretted because when I saw the pictures taken from that day, my head too closely resembled a bloated penis. Friends had the audacity to ask me—a woman pregnant with triplets in her second trimester—what the hell was I thinking? Answer: I wasn't.

With the help of several superhumanly strong people, I made my way onto the table in the doctor's office. My perinatologist was particularly chipper that day. I wasn't sure why, but I suspected that it could be because instead of being pregnant with triplets, he owned an adorable French cottage in Provence that he would visit throughout the year, jetting there whenever he liked. When not enjoying life in France, he rented it out for extra cash, which would never go towards diapers and formula, because he didn't have children. At that very moment, as I lay on my back unable to move from the large house I had bought myself on my abdomen, it felt like he was gloating over his superior life choices. I felt like wielding the girth of my giant body and mowing him down like a wrecking ball.

He lifted up my muumuu, took one look at my belly and said, "When you get done with this pregnancy, your belly is going to look like a map of the United States!" Then he laughed out loud. His LOL reverberated through my ugly penis hat and I looked at him in terror. My mind quickly flashed to the map of the United States that hung on the classroom wall in third grade. There were so many black and red lines all over that map; thin lines and thick lines, swirling lines and straight lines. All of a sudden I felt a little queasy. I inherited thighs prone to cellulite, and cankles that could be tracked through my British ancestry all the way back to Queen Elizabeth the first. But I had a great stomach—nice and flat with curves in just the right places. According to my doctor, after this pregnancy, my best body feature would soon be outlines of Arizona and Nevada with the Continental divide running just below my belly button.

As I lay flat out like a potbelly pig taking a nap, getting poked and prodded in my vaginal region for the 50th time in months, I daydreamed about how I got here. It went something like this:

Doctor: Are you sure you want to put four embryos in? They all look very good and viable.

Me: Of course I do! I don't want to keep going through this process for the next ten years of my life. I am going to put all of my eggs in one uterine basket! LOL! (I actually did laugh out loud at my own pun).

Doctor: What will you do if they all take? I don't believe in selective reduction.

Me: Oh, don't worry about that. I was told I would never get pregnant again with my under-achieving eggs. I'd be lucky to get one out of this deal.

Fast forward a few weeks and here were my pregnancy hormone BETA hCG levels:

Day 10 BETA 1: 153
Day 12 BETA 2: 416
Day 17 BETA 3: 1,692
Day 23 BETA 4: 10,503

These numbers were significantly higher than they would be if I were pregnant with one baby, so I was excited about having twins. I went to the fertility center to get my first ultrasound, and there they were up on the screen—three little sacs with huge beating hearts.

The ensuing conversation about my ultrasound finding went like this:

Doctor: Looks like you are having triplets.

Me: It's early. How do you know they will all make it? (Not that I didn't want them to make it, only because I had experienced two miscarriages and an ectopic pregnancy, so I was dubious.)

Doctor: Because their hearts are beating so strong. They *will* all make it.

Me: How do you know there isn't a fourth baby hiding behind one of the other ones?

Doctor: There isn't.

Me: But how do you know? Haven't you heard those stories of hiding fetuses before?

At 30 weeks pregnant, my husband shot a video of me at Starbucks. When I watch it now, I cringe at how miserable I was. I was absolutely the most miserable pregnant person alive at that moment—and there are a lot of miserable pregnant people out there. My entire body was swollen from head to toe. I could hardly eat because I had no room for food, yet I was perpetually starving. I was in pain. I could barely walk. I needed a scooter to get around Costco.

It was on this particular day at 30 weeks that I ended up in the hospital for my three-and-a-half-week stint. It never crossed my mind that I would share a room at the hospital. I required my personal space, especially at a time like this. When I found out there weren't enough beds to give me my own room, I threw a tantrum. I screamed and cried at the nurses and my husband, and acted exactly like a two-year old that didn't get to buy the toy she wanted from the store. Are you saying I have to be at my most vulnerable, miserable time in my life with a roommate I have never met?

My roommate was 29 weeks pregnant with twins. While my belly still looked pristine, like an overstretched water balloon, smooth and atlas-less, my roommate had not been as lucky. Her belly was covered in bright red stretch marks that seemed to glow like a neon sign. I don't know if she developed her gaseous problems in pregnancy or if she always ran a bit gassy, but she spent most days burping like a trucker, without apology. She must have burped a thousand times while we roomed together, and not once did I hear an "Excuse me."

During the three and a half weeks I spent in the hospital on bed rest, I needed to be monitored three times a day to make sure none of my babies were in distress. When I wasn't enduring a violation of my personal space by well-intentioned nurses, I had a lot of free time on my hands. When I was on hospital bed rest it was like the technological stone ages compared to today. There was no Facebook, Instagram or Twitter posting or browsing to kill time. I didn't even have a cell phone, and I used a laptop computer that may be eligible for placement in a museum today.

Without social media or proper technological devices, here's what I did:

- Watch nice long movies like *Anna Karenina*.

- Drink cranberry juice on ice through a straw.

- Eat grilled cheese sandwiches and Jell-O.

- Write.

- Listen to music on my iPod touch.

The truth is, being on hospital bed rest was relaxing. I did miss my family. I got lonely and grew tired of listening to my roommate burp, but being in the hospital gave me time to nurture my body. When I was at home, I felt like I needed to do things like cook and clean. My three-year-old would jump on me in a playful way and that didn't feel good with the litter that was growing inside me. In the hospital I got to do whatever I wanted all day long. I would ring the nurses whenever I needed my daily Jell-O shot. I could adjust the hospital bed until I was as comfortable as I could ever be in my condition. I wore my hospital robe, you know the one that ties in the back, every single day without exception. I barely combed my hair, which eventually formed impressive dreadlocks in the back part of my head. I could tell my appearance was embarrassing to my visitors, but I did not care. I was growing three babies.

My amazing cervix could have carried these babies to full term, as it was still closed up like a steel trap at 33 weeks. I'm not sure you could even get that thing open with a vice. Yet, my small body had called it quits. It was failing in a series of small ways under the pressure of housing three babies. There was a space issue in my womb, forcing my son up under my left ribs. This was causing me so much pain that I had to pop a pain pill one night. The next morning my perinatologist came into the room and told me I had come far enough and it was time to get the babies out that day.

I put makeup on my bloated face because I knew there would be many pictures taken of me on this monumental day. My family was gathered around my hospital bed where I lay almost as wide as I was long. My mom was nervous. I am sure she thought I could die somewhere along the way between carrying and delivering three babies at the same time.

They wheeled me into the hospital room at noon when my babies were exactly 33 ½ weeks (when you are pregnant with triplets you go by a gestational calendar). Instead of eating lunch, I would be evicting three babies from my body. The anesthesiologist was very sophisticated with his tall handsome looks and Tom Selleck mustache. He asked me to tell him when I could feel anything happening below the curtain—you know, like a scalpel slicing through my abdomen and organs being placed on the outside of my belly. I told him that I couldn't feel anything yet. He said, "Well, we are in! We have already made the incision and we are almost ready to pull the first baby out!" The pride of a pain-free job well done had him giddy; like this was the first C-section he had attended. I appreciated his enthusiasm under the circumstances.

Each baby was brought out within two minutes of each other. When they pulled my boy out from under my ribs, I made an audible "uhhhhhhhhhh" sound and I could hear the sucking of his body as he left his spot. I am sure neither one of us were comfortable with his position in the womb.

When you are expecting triplets, there are stories you hear along the way, and many of them are not encouraging. Would all my babies be healthy? Would they be able to breathe on their own? Would they all be whisked away by busy nurses trying to save their tiny lives? So when the nurse brought me all three of my babies to hold, I was shocked. I held them and looked into their perfect faces. I loved them already. I loved them in a profoundly special way, because we had all fought a good fight to be there in that moment. It certainly wasn't easy for any of us.

The night after I delivered my triplets, I could not sleep. I got up in the middle of the night all doped up on Norco, and had a nurse wheel me into the NICU so I could hold my babies. By the time I got up to the NICU in my wheelchair, I was nodding off and bleeding like a woman who has been shot, drugged and left for dead.

Many triplet pregnancies do not end well, and I believe part of my incredible excitement to see my babies that night was that they were healthy. It could have been bad. My babies could have died. I could have died. The human body is not built to endure such a heavy burden.

But guess what? There is no map of the United States on my belly. So stamp that on your passport and stick it up your French chateau, perinatologist!

Megan Woolsey is a writer, editor and publisher living in Northern California with a very supportive husband and a wild bunch of red-headed children - a set of triplets and their big sister. Megan has been published in Huffington Post, Scary Mommy, BLUNTmoms, Bonbon Break, Mamalode, In The Powder Room and is an essayist in two anthologies.

PREGNANCY

BELLY TALK

JANET MCNALLY

Let's talk about the belly. This was the most remarkable thing about my twin pregnancy, and I'm using that word with the following definition: "of or like a spectacle." It was a spectacle, my belly. And so was I.

But not in the beginning. In the beginning, I had only a small bump, though even then it was bigger than it had been during my first pregnancy. I figured that was just the way it went the second time around. Before I was comfortable telling everyone, I hid it as best I could with a complicated array of scarves and loose sweaters. I held objects in front of my belly: a sack of groceries, my 16-month-old daughter. At my second visit, my midwife asked if I might be further along than I thought. "Your uterus is higher than I'd expect," she said. Why the possibility of twins did not occur to me (or her), I do not know. My grandmother had two sets, but to be fair that was out of 13 children total and, since then, no one else, not my aunts nor my cousins, had a set of twins. I did not expect to win that lottery.

I won that lottery.

When the sonographer said, "How do you feel about two?" and I saw on the screen two babies floating in space in their separate amniotic sacs, the first thing I said was, "No." Which isn't an accurate answer to that question, but was the first word that came to my mind. Then, beyond that word, the first thing I thought about was not my belly. It was my car. Or the fact that we were going to have to get a new one. A car that could fit three children. Maybe a—gasp—minivan? The whole situation suddenly seemed like a math equation. It was a matter of space.

"How am I going to fit two babies at a time in my body?" I asked the sonographer, gesturing a little wildly at my torso. "I'm a pretty small person."

She was kind. She smiled. "Bodies find a way," she said. I'm here to report that, yes, they do. That way is *out*. That way is *sphere*. That way is *bloom* and *push* and *stretch*. My hips and pelvis shifted like the gears of a clock, and I realized that my body had been full of beautiful, complicated machinery this whole time. I just didn't know it.

This is true of any pregnancy, sure, but having done it with a single baby first, I recognized quickly that a twin pregnancy was a whole other ballgame, not least because what was inside me was basically an octopus, eight limbs poking in all directions. A beloved, two-headed, two-bodied octopus, but still.

I've never been so aware of gravity in my life. My belly had its own gravity, tipping me forward, drawing the glances of everyone I passed. At the college where I teach, crowds parted for me—literally. Heads turned my way as if I were an astronomical event. People ran to open doors for me.

"Your body just doesn't make sense," one of my students said. "I mean, it's beautiful, a miracle, whatever. But how does it do that?"

"Your guess is as good as mine," I said. Then: "Magic."

It did feel like magic. And just like in a fairy tale, magic always comes with a price. For me, that price was twofold, two kinds of worry. The first was the important one: worry about whether the girls would be born healthy and safe. That was what really mattered; I always knew that. Still, I couldn't keep the other kind of worry from nipping at my heels: the fear that my body would never be the same, that it would be ruined somehow.

My high-risk-pregnancy doctor had a vinyl recliner that felt like a cloud. I wanted to sit in that chair all day, and not only because it was so comfortable. In that chair, one of the worries went away. I could hear my girls' heartbeats gallop around each other like the hoof-beat soundtrack to a spaghetti Western, and I knew they were safe. I could forget about gravity, sort of, and pretend I was floating in midair. But there was no way to forget about the half-moon shape of my belly, rising in front of me.

I carried my girls for more than 38 weeks and, even then, I had to be induced. They wanted to stay longer, their limbs tucked around their bodies, petals around a budding flower, tapping Morse code messages from the inside of my abdomen. But after a whole day of waiting, hooked up to an IV of Pitocin, and two hours of pushing, both babies came into the world. The first was taken away immediately because I was still pushing, and when her sister was born (an hour and 20 minutes later), I was shocked when they put that slimy, beautiful baby on my belly. On the outside, her limbs unfurled, the flower blooming.

After that, my body became my own again, in a way. I was nursing, so the babies were still attached to me, but I could put them down from time to time. I could walk across a room alone. I don't remember what it felt like, those first few days, to be free from that belly. To be a girl again, and not some sort of moon. My uterus was contracting, and my bones were shifting back, trying to remember where they'd been before. They eventually found their way back, mostly. I learned to walk without tipping forward, and though I still live by the rules of gravity, I don't think about that elemental force very often.

I had a diastasis, which commonly happens when your abdominal muscles are stretched apart too far, though it can be mostly corrected with exercise and binding. It's true that the skin of my belly will never be the same smooth, taut surface it was before, though, so I guess one of my fears came true. My body is not the same, and I'll certainly never be a bikini model. I'll probably never wear a bikini again. At first that felt like a disaster. But in the last two years, it's come to matter much less. What matters more is the two other healthy bodies I carried for nearly nine months, my girls, who are becoming taller and stronger every day.

My belly was a moon, or maybe a planet all its own, with only two inhabitants, both tiny girls. And now they live somewhere else, with me on the outside, but my belly remembers where they used to live, and I do, too.

Janet McNally is the author of the YA novel, Girls in the Moon, *coming in Fall 2016 from HarperCollins/ HarperTeen, and a collection of poems,* Some Girls, *winner of the White Pine Press Poetry Prize. She has an MFA from the University of Notre Dame and has twice been a fiction fellow with the New York Foundation for the Arts. Janet lives with her husband and three little girls (including twins) in Buffalo, where she teaches creative writing at Canisius College.*

JOURNAL IT
_____

Write your thoughts and feelings down. Capture the moments. Life with multiples is exciting and busy, and it's easy to forget the little things and details. Here are some writing prompts to help you along.

Pregnancy is a wondrous thing. A multiples pregnancy is even more so. How do you feel about your body?

What are your favorite memories from when you were pregnant with twins/ triplets/ more?

PREGNANCY

LABOR AND DELIVERY

PREGNANCY

WHAT TO PACK FOR THE HOSPITAL

MEGAN WOOLSEY

When I was 30 weeks pregnant with triplets, I was admitted to the hospital for the rest of my pregnancy. I had been doing too much that day—which wasn't a lot—but when you have a 40-pound bowling ball on your abdomen, every step is an exertion. When I began to feel my contractions at a regular clip, we knew it was time to go to the hospital.

I should have been more prepared for this moment, the one where because I am pregnant with multiples, I unexpectedly end up in the hospital. Instead, we were forced to pack a bag in less than five minutes. I was sitting in the car waiting while Chris threw some clothes (which I never wore) and a few toiletries into a bag. Little did I know that this was not a practice run—the hospital would be my home for the next three and a half weeks until I delivered my babies.

There were many items that trickled into my hospital room over the next several days to make me comfortable for my extended stay on the third floor of Sutter General Hospital. Those first few days were lonely and scary as I lay in my bed with strangers poking and prodding me like a Thanksgiving turkey at all hours of the day and night.

There were things that my family and friends brought me during my stay that were a beautiful reminder that I was not alone and I did not have to feel as if I were in a foreign land.

Pack a bag with these items and you will be ready for a comfortable stay at the hospital:

- A smartphone with a playlist of your favorite songs (My sister made me a playlist of awesome songs and put them on my iPod Touch. To this day when I listen to those songs, I have strong memories of my hospital stay).

- An extension cord and a cell phone charger.

- Don't assume you will have Internet connections. Call your hospital to find out. If you don't have good connections, make sure you have music streaming service available offline.

- Magazines, books and movies (My hospital room had an old-school television with a DVD player attached, so I had friends bring me movies.)

- Earplugs (There is a *lot* of noise in hospitals)

- A laptop or tablet

- A couple of nursing bras if you plan to breastfeed

- Nice-smelling lotions and lip balm for when you get dry

- Baggy button-down shirt for easy access, if breastfeeding

- A few pairs of extra large or stretchy underwear

- A comfortable robe

- Your favorite soap

- A camera

- Your own pillow

- A cozy blanket

- A few pairs of comfortable and warm socks

- Extra roomie backless slippers that your feet slide into, in case they are retaining water and swollen

- Good quality feminine pads

- Dry shampoo

- A pacifier for each baby

- Snacks (My brother-in-law worked for Pepperidge Farms and he brought me a big box of crackers and cookies for my hospital room.)

- Note pads for thank you cards while you have time (before the babies come home!)

When my babies were in the NICU they wore diapers only and spent their days wrapped in blankets. They did not wear any outfits, kind of like me during my stay in the hospital (I only wore the hospital gown for three and a half weeks). Therefore, find out how much you need for the babies in the event they have a NICU stay.

Moms of multiples recommend bringing a packed bag to every doctor's appointment after 20 weeks. There is a likelihood you will end up being sent from the doctor's office to the hospital if they find you are dilated or having contractions, or if one or more babies are in distress.

Now you are prepared for your hospital stay!

OUTPLAN

JACKIE PICK

When I was nine months pregnant with twins, my life revolved around naps, chips and salsa, and occasional bon mots about how life was about to change. After all, it's easy to navel-gaze when your belly button is parallel with your eyes. I used my doctor-ordered bed rest as an opportunity to contemplate my identity and my future as a mother, both immediate and long term. Daily marathons of *A Baby Story* helped me visualize my ideal labor and delivery, although ultimately I was fine with any birthing scenario that did not resemble the burst-from-the-chest scene from *Alien*. The next 18 years promised chaos, so I wanted the first three or four days of being a newly minted family of four to be as peaceful, warm, and intimate as possible.

At 36 weeks, my mucus plug unceremoniously popped out as I was getting a reload of Tostitos. My husband expressed mild interest in this event (by which I mean he looked up from his computer), but not enough to examine the evidence. I waddled to the bathroom to freshen up, confident that a lost plug meant babies were imminent, much like if I'd lost the cap to an air mattress. I assumed there'd be a prolonged rude noise, then complete deflation of my belly, then babies.

For four days the babies remained imminent while I sat around plug-less and baby-less. I worried that the twins were in utero without the cap on tightly, at risk of spoiling and coming out curdled. In desperation, I consulted the Internet to crowdsource ways to speed things along. The next several hours involved pseudo-yoga poses, cartwheels, and cooking something called "birthing chicken." I was about to give my husband a spoonful of castor oil—hey, he wanted to be part of the experience—when he suggested I untwist myself and call it a night.

I put my hair up in a style that can only be described as "Scare the Neighbors" and pulled on a tank top and a pair of my husband's SpongeBob silk boxers, declaring myself most decidedly not having babies that night. Husband and dog joined me by my side and feet, respectively.

When you have more than one baby in your belly, you create exactly 5,782 more gallons of amniotic fluid than a singleton pregnancy. At 1:37 a.m., I woke to a popping noise and a release of pressure as though a balloon filled with warm, slimy fluid had been punched out of me. My water didn't break, it unleashed…all over the dog.

With a start, I yelled, "Holy shit, my water just broke!" I jumped out of bed, hoping one of the babies' heads would act like a cork and stop the gush. It didn't.

Like a big dummy wearing SpongeBob boxers, I hopped around grabbing my crotch, as one does when one is about to bring forth life. My husband fetched a towel and swaddled my nether regions. I was his first diapering experience.

After pointless attempts to dry off the bed, the carpet, and the dog, we headed for the car. The dog, damp and insulted, slammed the door behind us.

My husband and I spent a majority of the drive to the hospital bickering. "Slow down! It's raining!" I nagged like a sitcom housewife.

"Are you kidding?" He noted that there are not many times his wife would be in labor at 2:15 in the morning while wearing one of his terrycloth origami creations. "I practically have a free pass to speed."

I distracted myself from his recklessness by calling my parents to tell them the babies were coming. By the time I hung up the phone 30 seconds later, they were already at the hospital. They had been prepping for the babies' arrival, too; my mother had been going to bed fully dressed for weeks.

My husband's breakneck speed got us to the hospital in exactly the same amount of time it always took us. We were met at the door by the overnight concierge, who had been hired right out of the icy grip of Death. This poor older gentleman broke out in a sweat trying to push my wheelchair over the threshold. He rebuked my husband's efforts to take over the driving, using the effortful trip down the hallway as a challenge not to break a hip. I was afraid I was going to give birth in the foyer four hours later and three inches from where we entered.

After the grueling 40-yard marathon to the nurses' station, I was handed a natty little paper gown and directed to a laboring room. The laboring room, which doubled as a broom closet during dips in population growth, quickly turned into the crowded cabin scene from *A Night at the Opera*, with people standing glove-to-glove, all straining to get a good look at me beached on the bed.

I was subjected to multiple interrogations by medical students while my contractions intensified. Or perhaps the constant questions intensified my contractions. In either case, it felt as though someone was squeezing my intestines and dropping an anvil on my chest while asking me my date of birth. My brain wired itself directly to my belly and my lungs, and I was sure my body was preparing to turn inside out. Soon, the questions and my body found a certain rhythm.

"Date of birth?" Contraction. "Last OB visit?" Contraction. "Position of babies?" Contraction. "Date of birth?" Contraction. "Oh, hey, what's your date of birth?"

A group of doctors, nurses, and probably janitors performed multiple physical exams while I gave Med Student Number 42 my information again. I achieved Birthing Level:

Muppet when Med Student Number 43 kneaded my cervix as I gave out my birthdate for the fourteenth time, waved to my parents who were sticking their heads in every three seconds, and also answered the anesthesiologist's questions about my allergies in a squeaky voice. At this point, my nose lit up like the guy on the Operation game board, and a new medical pit crew came in to take their turn.

A resident crammed into the room to perform a tenth cervical exam, which was free because I got my card punched after the first nine. "You're already five centimeters," she paused and made a face. "I just felt a foot." I assume she meant one of the babies', but I'm no expert in anatomy. "Yep, you just delivered a foot and ankle. We have to get these babies out. Now." I was wheeled from the laboring room to the impossibly more crowded operating room, where all multiples were delivered.

It was time for my doctor to arrive, the one who knew my history, my barfing-on-the-table phobia, my babies, and my tendency to make terrible jokes when I'm nervous. However, she'd been called out of town, so her partner, whom I'd never met, snapped on her gloves and stepped in. I introduced myself to her with as much dignity as I could muster while naked and hunching over a nurse so I could receive my epidural in this excruciatingly well-lit space.

Once the epidural hit, I had space in my own body again. I watched, immobilized except for my uncontrollable shakes, as my twins' medical teams came in. It was standing room only, and soon enough two more little people would join us.

You may be asking yourself, as I was in very colorful language, where my husband was. He was the only person within a four-mile radius not in this reverse-clown car of a room. Like every first-time father, he was off getting a sandwich, having heard from his medically reliable poker buddies that first births can take upwards of seven weeks. A nurse was dispatched to find him.

Finally, my husband was shoved in the room by what I assume was a Japanese subway packer. I asked him if he'd washed his hands. The doctor gave a pity laugh, at which my husband jumped.

"Hi, Charlie," said the beautiful young doctor, her eyes blazing from behind her mask. Ever the bright one, I asked, "Do you know each other?" I could tell by the way my husband shifted in his shoes that they shared quite a history.

I made a mental note to cross "Have husband's ex-girlfriend take a gander at my privates while she removes two babies from my bulging midsection" off my bucket list. Visions of a wonky C-section scar that spelled out "he never called me back" flashed before my eyes.

By the time the doctor uttered the words, "You're going to feel some tugging," Baby A was out. Who was that squirmy little mole rat they were holding up? They held him up to me for approval, like a bottle wine. "Cute," I said, not entirely convinced, but he was my mole rat and I loved him.

Baby B followed two minutes later, with no cry. It was the first of a lifetime of worried moments. He was whisked off for oxygen and brought back moments later, pink and confused. I nuzzled my two little mole rats. "Hello," I said. "Remember it's your birthday, because some day, 400 people will ask you."

Waiting in recovery to feel like something other than a block of marble, I watched my husband hold our sons. The boys quickly resumed womb life by curling into each other, intertwining, sticking hands in faces without complaint. They were each other's first touch. Months ago their hearts began beating together. They would be each other's longest relationship. I marveled at my sudden sense of place and time.

I asked my husband for a moment of privacy so I could fight back tears and also possibly throw up from the anesthesia.

Once I recovered and got feeling back in my arms and legs, I held my babies for the first time. I'd never held a baby before, never mind two, so they rested in my arms at unnatural, rakish angles, but they forgave me and fell asleep while I wondered if I was looking at them equally enough.

I changed my first, second, and millionth diapers those first few days in hospital. I was terrible at it, but gave myself credit for diapering the correct end. I learned quickly that twins often cry at the same time, and occasionally one will just have to cry longer while I attended to his brother. It's unfair, but sometimes being a multiple means you're not removed from your own poop on demand.

My own doctor returned the next morning at 5:30 and approved of how the babies were born. She hadn't dated my husband, so she busied herself (not glaring at him) while prodding my belly.

My doctor was followed by a parade of hospital workers, completely different than the workers who had populated my labor and delivery rooms. I'm convinced that hospitals are employing 97% of Americans. They came in and checked me, my scars, my mental health, and my maxi pad. I had not planned for so many people to be rooting around in my panties. I began automatically lowering my mesh drawers for anyone who walked in. This led to a hastily issued apology to the man from the garage who had just wanted to clear up a parking fee.

Conversations with my husband those first few days were brief, as I was loopy from drugs and Gas-X, and he was exhausted from sleeping in a glorified folding chair. He'd squint at me and ask, "You okay?"

"Yeah," I'd answer, wincing from the baby gums clamping down like the jaws of life on my nipples. "Cool." It was like our wedding vows all over again.

These declarations were strengthened by the maternity nurses. These angels of mercy were so determined to increase the levels of intimacy in my marriage that they would ask me right in front of my husband whether I'd pooped yet. We'd kept this particular area of my life a mystery up until that time. He, in what I can only assume was an attempt to co-parent, was more than happy to share his digestive track's status with the nurses. The nurses eventually stopped coming into my room, opting instead to open the door a crack and toss me some Dulcolax. Picking up the slack were the lactation consultants, ever at the ready and living by the motto, "No Part of My Boobs Left Untouched." There were many of them, they were eager, and they never seemed to communicate with one another that I had figured out the feeding thing by the eighteenth nursing tutorial. Lactation consultants make up the other 3% of the American workforce.

Efforts to catch some sleep were thwarted by all friends and family in the tri-state area stopping by to bring flowers, peek at the babies, and marvel at how big they were. This was admittedly a welcome change from people marveling at how big I had been while pregnant. Although some troublemakers couldn't hide their glances at my belly to see if I'd already lost all the pregnancy weight, however, most visitors just wanted to say hi and not offer to babysit. Close family and friends wanted to play "Whose Side of the Family?" which involved firmly planting each claim on the appropriate branch of the family tree. The game blithely ignored the fact that both babies looked like Winston Churchill suppressing a belch. I made the mistake of suggesting that the boys each looked like a combination of the two families, igniting a feud that to this day means spending hours on strategic Thanksgiving seating charts.

After five days, the nurses kindly reminded us that this wasn't actually a hotel, and that we needed to vacate the premises. We bundled up the boys warmly enough to brave whatever freak blizzard might hit that August day. We headed out, our family of four. I had 87 bouquets of flowers tucked into the wheelchair with me. I looked like the world's only mobile floral shop with hemorrhoids. Charlie and the babies were right beside me. It was just us now. Just us, two diaper bags, three suitcases, countless sets of instructions, one giant big rig double stroller, extra pads, blankets, hospital burping towels, and one nurse trying to take one last look in my maxi pad.

After only 45 minutes of figuring out how to get everything in the car (my Tetris obsession finally paid off!), I gingerly turned around in my seat to gaze at my beautiful babies who were busy spitting up all over the brand new car seats. And I realized…

…it had all gone according to plan.

Jackie Pick is a former teacher who is now writing her way through what she nervously identifies as her "second adolescence." Her work can be found in The HerStories Project anthology: So Glad They Told Me *(Spring, 2016) and on* Scary Mommy. *She is the co-creator and co-writer of the upcoming short film* Bacon Wrapped Dates, *and occasionally performs in and directs sketch comedy in Chicago. When she's not in one of her three children's school pick-up lanes, she can be found on Twitter apologizing for not updating her blog.*

WHAT'S THE TIME?

_____

ALISON LEE

"3:00 a.m."

My eyes flicker open, as I feel a slight gush. A gush that no pregnant woman at 34 weeks wants to feel. This is my third pregnancy; I know what it means.

Less than 24 hours ago at my weekly checkup my obstetrician advised bed rest because I was having contractions I couldn't even feel. He gave me an injection to "calm the uterus" and sent me on my way, confident as I was that I would take this twin pregnancy to full-term, 37 weeks.

Pulling myself up, I walk to the bathroom and sit down on the toilet, trying to tell myself that the gush was just pee. Yes, of course. How silly of me. I go back to bed.

Oh. It's happening again. This time, faster, heavier. Up I go again and leave a trail of amniotic fluid on the floor.

"No. NO. NONONONONONO." I try to will my body to stop this nonsense. Thirty-four weeks is too soon. Thirty-four weeks means possible respiratory issues for the babies. Thirty-four weeks most certainly means that they will be tiny, which in turn spells NICU, something my doctor had explicitly stated that, ideally, it's what we want to avoid. Silently, I chastise my body. We had a deal, Womb! Carry these babies to term! Or least for another week. Come on!

The flow of fluid comes faster, and by the time I reach my husband—still sleeping and blissfully unaware of what was to come—I am crying, waddling with a towel between my legs. I shake him awake.

"My water's broken. We have to go to the hospital now."

He leaps out of bed, alarmed by my tears, still not comprehending the enormity of the situation (in my mind at least). As he calls his mother to come over to watch our older boys, I get dressed and start throwing random things into my diaper bag. The bag that was unpacked because 34 weeks is too soon.

I reach into the babies' closet and grab some clothes and swaddling blankets, the thought that they wouldn't even need them for the first 10 days of their lives not even crossing my mind. I'm giving birth to these babies today so they'll need clothes and swaddling blankets. I text my doctor, "My water broke. Heading to the hospital now." He replies, "OK." I take that calmness as a good sign. We're going to be fine.

The 10 minutes it takes my mother-in-law to arrive feels like an eternity. I have no appreciation of what a Herculean effort it must have been for her—woken in the middle of the night, told that her grandchildren were coming too soon, get dressed, hurry over and appear calm and collected to her already-panicked daughter-in-law.

Yes, I feel panicky. The contractions are intense and close together. Too soon or not, these babies are coming.

"4:00 a.m."

I half-walk, half-waddle to the reception at the emergency room, and hand over an emergency admittance sheet that I'd never thought I'd need. "Thirty-four weeks" was running on repeat in my head.

As I am wheeled to the labor ward at a speed I feel does not match the rate at which my body is trying to expel my twins, I say a silent prayer.

I heave onto the bed, and a midwife does a cervix check. Concerned faces surround me, and they give me an injection "for the babies' lungs."

"Where's my doctor?"

I know where he is. My doctor is in surgery, delivering another set of 34-week-old twins via a scheduled C-section. I remember he told me this yesterday at my checkup, which seems like a million years ago.

"NURSE! Please, I can feel the baby coming," Panic underlying my false calm.

They wheel me to the operating room, right next to the other mother, delivering her too-small twins, while I resist the forces of nature, trying to evacuate my too-small twins from my body. I am fighting tooth and nail, to no avail. I can feel a baby's head. There is no one in the OR, except for the midwife from the labor ward who thought to come with me.

"Where's everyone? Why isn't there a sense of urgency?" I ask. She tells me that everyone is next door; they'll be here soon.

"I think you need to get someone, he or she is coming NOW." I sound far too calm to my ears. She checks me and suddenly snaps into action. "Call someone now," she booms to an orderly.

I recognize the lady who walks in, despite the mask on her face, and her bloody gown. She's an obstetrician who practices out of the same clinic as my doctor. I greet her, and she seems surprised that I know who she is. My doctor walks in next, gets briefed. For the first time, I hear the midwife who was with me from the start say, "She's fully dilated."

I see a digital clock on the wall, which reads "15:40" and it doesn't strike me as strange though I know that it is early morning. I focus on the clock, and its numbers, trying to ignore the flurry of action around me. My doctor is telling me things—we don't have any ventilators; they're all utilized; we might have to transfer you to another hospital; blah blah blah. I refuse to absorb the potentially bad news.

I look away from the clock and focus on what's happening to my body. I've done this before; I've got this. My babies are coming, whether I'm ready or not. Thirty-four weeks or not. Too soon or not. They're coming.

They tell me to lie back, open my legs and push. There is no time for transfers and such. Fear grips me. No ventilators. They expect my babies to have respiratory issues. Of course, their lungs are not fully developed at this stage.

I feel an enormous pressure inside of me, and focus on the female doctor's voice. She says push. I do. Primal instinct takes over. I push again, feeling that intense burning sensation, then relief. I hear my baby's loud cry. Does that mean that his or her lungs are okay? I ask, is that the girl? The doctor tells me she didn't check. She'd handed him or her off immediately to a team from NICU. I can see them working on my baby from the corner of my eye.

"Alison, you have to do this again. We have to get your other baby out now. Wait for a contraction, and push."

Again, I look at the clock; it says "15:50." I still don't find it strange. For some reason, my brain is registering the time as 5:50 a.m. When I last checked the time, it was 4 a.m. Has it been two hours?

No time to think. Time to work. I push. And push again. Twin Two flies out, along with other bodily fluids. Someone says it's a boy. I don't remember hearing a cry. Did he cry? I hope he cried.

I feel spent. I push again, and out pops the placenta. The female doctor who caught both babies tells me I need one stitch, and she's going to do it without painkillers. I say, okay, sure.

That needle hurt more than labor.

"Where's my husband?" I ask various people, as I head to recovery. No one seems to know. How strange, I think. Where did he go? The last time I saw him was just before I was wheeled into the operating room when he told me he had to park the car in the garage. He'd left it where we'd screeched to a stop earlier, outside the emergency room. I am anxious that he has no idea what just happened.

The female doctor comes to check on me after what seems like an eternity. My obsession with time isn't over. I ask about the babies, and she tells me that they are in the NICU. Not for the first time, fear flinches in my heart.

"Are they okay?"

"Yes! But, you need to talk to the neonatologist, he'll come by to see you later."

I ask about my husband. She kindly offers to call him on her cell phone. After she briefs him (Congratulations on the twins! They are alive, as is your wife!), she hands the phone to me. He explains that he'd been outside the OR, and no one told him what happened despite his desperate efforts at finding out. He was hanging about the labor ward waiting for an update. I tell him, go to the NICU. Check on the babies. I'll see you later.

As she fills out paperwork, I overhear her tell a coworker that my first baby was born at 4:47 a.m., and her brother, at 4:59 a.m. I think about that clock in the operating room— why was it wrong? Why did I not think it was strange at the time? I wonder why I am fixating on the clock. Was it so I wouldn't freak out about my preemies?

I need to know how my babies are.

"Let them be okay. Let them be okay. Let them be okay."

"9:30 a.m."

I finally lay eyes on my babies, feel their smooth skin, and marvel at these tiny human beings. My tiny human beings. They are okay. They are okay. They are okay.

Alison Lee is the co-editor of Multiples Illuminated, *a writer, and publisher. A former PR and marketing professional, she is the owner of Little Love Media, specializing in blog book tours. Alison's writing has been featured in Mamalode, On Parenting at The Washington Post, The Huffington Post, Everyday Family, Scary Mommy, and Club Mid. She is one of 35 essayists in the anthology,* My Other Ex: Women's True Stories of Leaving and Losing Friends *(Fall, 2014), and has an essay in another,* So Glad They Told Me: Women Get Real About Motherhood *(Spring, 2016). She is also an editor at BonBon Break, an online magazine. Alison lives in Malaysia with her husband and four children (two boys and boy/girl twins).*

JOURNAL IT

Write your thoughts and feelings down. Capture the moments. Life with multiples is exciting and busy, and it's easy to forget the little things and details. Here is a writing prompt to help you along.

Write your birth story.

NEONATAL INTENSIVE CARE UNIT (NICU)

NAVIGATING THE NICU

ALISON LEE

Expectant mothers of multiples face the possibility that their babies could be born prematurely. It's an ongoing goal for both mothers and their health care providers to maintain the pregnancy for as long as possible to ensure healthy outcomes for the babies.

The first major milestone is 24 weeks, the threshold of viability. These micro-preemies typically spend at least three months in the NICU.

The next milestone is 28 weeks, where 90% of babies who make it to this stage survive. Their NICU stay is usually two to three months, and long-term complications are still possible.

Multiples born at 32 to 34 weeks have the best odds of survival, with minimal long-term complications. A stay at the NICU remains a possibility though because babies at this stage usually do not have lung maturity, and need help breathing. At this prematurity stage, babies are often fed through a feeding tube. NICU stays for late-term preemies range from two weeks or longer; my 34-weekers were in the NICU for two weeks, mostly so they could gain weight.

Most people view the NICU as a scary place, but it is the best place for your preemies. Neonatal medical care is technologically advanced. The doctors and nurses who work in neonatal care about your babies, and they work hard for your children. Learn to trust them.

Here are some best practices to help you navigate the NICU.

- See your babies in the NICU as soon as you're physically able. Being separated from them immediately after delivery is difficult. Facing the NICU as soon as possible is also the best way to come to terms with the fact that your multiples need to be there.

- Get to know your babies' neonatologist and pediatric nurses. You'll be seeing a lot of them, and you want them on your side.

- Familiarize yourself with the ins and outs of the NICU: the sanitization process, what all the machines attached to your babies are and what they do, and what it means when alarms go off (it's not always serious, sometimes it could just be a cord that comes loose or detached).

- Be involved in your babies' care as soon as you are allowed to. Changing diapers, bathing and feeding your babies give some normalcy to early-day parenting in a very trying situation.

- Practice kangaroo care as soon as possible, and frequently. Skin-to-skin contact does wonders for babies.

- Don't be afraid to ask questions. No question is stupid or unnecessary.

- If you're allowed to, personalize the room or area where your babies are. It's temporarily home for your babies, and you'll be spending a lot of time there.

- Don't forget your spouse. Visit the NICU together whenever possible. Give him some alone time with the babies.

- Advocate for your babies. If you feel that something is not right with their care, their health or information is not forthcoming, don't be afraid to ask, challenge, and question, until you get answers.

- While my twins were in NICU, I was able to recover quickly from my delivery. If you've had a C-section, this is an excellent time to rest and heal, knowing that your babies are in good hands. I was also able to spend time with my older two children.

- The NICU experience will have its ups and downs, especially if your multiples are micro- or early-term preemies. Stay positive, and gather your support system around you.

It's not desirable to have to leave your babies in the NICU, but remember that they are there to get better and grow stronger. Arm yourself with knowledge and a positive attitude, and you will bring your precious babies home soon.

SMALL COMFORTS

JANINE KOVAC

My postpartum room looks like a cinder block, gray and grimy and nothing like the bright, sunny antepartum room where I've spent the last 10 days. Just this morning I was so sure that that I'd be here for at least seven or eight more weeks. My twins were mono-chorionic/mono-amniotic, which meant they shared the same placenta and amniotic sac. It also meant that there was nothing to keep their umbilical cords from braiding together and cutting off their lifeline to food and oxygen.

The doctors had planned to induce me at 32 weeks, the point when the odds for survival outside the womb are greater than my twins' chances of surviving inside. However, my twins had another plan. Instead of eight weeks early, they decided to come 15 weeks early.

I'm too woozy from my emergency C-section to complain about my dirty room. Besides, I overheard one of the nurses say that it's overcrowded, and they'll have to double up some of the moms. The last thing I want is to share a room with a mom who just gave birth to a healthy full-term baby. This room may be small and gloomy, but at least I have it to myself. Maybe the nurses will let my husband sleep in the extra bed, the way he was allowed to stay in my antepartum room. Every night last week, after tucking our three-year-old daughter in for the night and leaving her in Nonna's care, Matt rushed back to the hospital to sleep on the pullout couch in my room.

"Just rest." The nurse tells me. She pats my hand. "You can meet your sons tomorrow." She flicks off the light and closes the door behind her.

Matt is with the twins in the NICU, somewhere I've never been, even though my doctor urged me to take a tour last week, gently suggesting I familiarize myself with the place.

"You might want to see what a preemie this small looks like. We have a baby that's just a couple of weeks older than your twins. A 26-weeker!" He told me proudly, the way a car salesman tells you about the new models.

"Looking at a 26-weeker is like looking at a car wreck," I retort. "It's not going to make me a safer driver."

He shrugged. "Some people want to know what they are in for."

That should have been my clue that he knew something I didn't about my pregnancy. I'd read about preemies, but I studied the information the same way one prepares for a test one assumes she won't have to take.

Tonight my doctor is happy. He says they'll never know for sure why I went into labor at 25 weeks, but Baby A (the one I called "the Red Baby" in utero) was born with his umbilical cord wrapped twice around the neck. His brother Baby B (the one I dubbed "the Blue Baby") was born with a knot in his umbilical cord. The doctor doesn't have to say it; the message is clear: if I hadn't had an emergency C-section just now, the twins wouldn't have made it.

The next morning the nurse takes my temperature and checks my stitches. Matt stands behind her with an empty wheelchair he found at the nurses' station. He stands very tall and still and I can tell he's trying not to pace. I have a groggy memory of him coming into the room around midnight, crashing in the armchair instead of the extra bed. It's only eight in the morning, but he's already been to the NICU twice today.

Matt wheels my chair through the double doors and past the NICU security desk. I'm pretty sure I can walk by myself, but no one else agrees with me, so I concede, but only because I'll get to the NICU faster if I hitch a ride.

There are teddy bear paintings on the walls and pastel curtains leading into each room. So we can pretend that this is a nursery and not a ward of life-support machines.

"You must scrub with anti-bacterial soap for 30 seconds each time you come into the NICU," the nurse says.

"NICU?" Matt repeats. Only he pronounces it "nee-coo" instead of "nick-you."

"Nick-you," I mutter, exasperated. This the third time today I've corrected him. Why can't he remember?

Matt turns to the nurse for verification. "Is it nee-coo or nick-you? Nee-coo? Neeee-coooo?"

"NICK-you," she confirms. She motions down the hall. "Your boys are in Room 3."

We wash our hands at the sinks, lathering up to the elbows like the stick figures in the diagrams.

"Why do you keep asking that?" I hiss. "It's NICK-you. NICK-you."

He shrugs, his eyes twinkling. "I just think nee-COO sounds better. I'm hoping if I say it enough, nee-COO will catch on." The last time he shaved was two weeks go, but his goofy grin still shines through his scraggly beard.

The boys share a long, narrow room together, one of the few in the NICU with floor-to-ceiling windows. Outside I can see the gray sidewalks slick with winter rain.

"Keep it together," I tell myself.

As soon as I see Baby B, I recognize my Blue Baby. Under the bilirubin lights, I can hardly see his bruises. It's as if he has already healed. Isn't that what they told us? That babies were more resilient than we gave them credit for?

The Blue Baby is in a Plexiglas box as if he is a specimen. He is supposed to be cloaked in darkness, surrounded by water, floating in an anti-gravity environment to strengthen muscles and joints. Human beings were never meant to live in a plastic box. Even if that plastic box keeps them alive.

This is the most unnatural thing in the world.

I push the thought away as soon as it passes through my mind. If I let the fear in, I will dissolve. There is too much to do. I have a little girl at home who needs attention, a husband who needs emotional support, and an extended family that needs information and reassurance. If my boys are going to make it, it will only be thanks to this state-of-the-art neonatal technology. I have to change my way of thinking.

Matt, who spent most of last night shuttling back and forth between the boys and me, explains the way the NICU works. Our babies, who weighed just over a pound and a half apiece, are micro-preemies. Their condition is so critical that each baby has a personal nurse who stands over him for every minute of her eight-hour shift. She is replaced by a "meal-breaker" during her half-hour lunch and both of her 15-minute breaks. When the boys' breathing stops or slows, the nurses adjust the oxygen levels.

"Our first obstacle is blood pressure," The Blue Baby's nurse says. Behind her machines beep and hum.

She hands me papers to sign.

"This one is a consent form for blood transfusions. That one is for banked breast milk."

Maybe it was the way she handed me the papers. Maybe it was the way she wouldn't make eye contact. Matt was here last night. Why didn't he sign these? And why is the nurse acting strangely? I get a sinking feeling. Yesterday I signed a consent form to have a C-section 30 minutes after the fact.

"You want me to sign a consent form for the C-section I already had?" I asked the doctor.

She raised her eyebrows. "When lives are in danger, we do the paperwork later."

Back in the NICU, I look at the Blue Baby and then at his nurse.

"What would have happened if they needed a blood transfusion yesterday and I hadn't signed this form yet?"

"Well, we just gave it to them. They needed it."

I purposely avoid looking at Matt. If I do, I'll see him realize what is just dawning on me: they've already had a round of blood transfusions. If we lock eyes, I know I'll see my fear reflected in his face. This is our new normal; we don't have time for fear. He turns away from me, too.

Instead, I look at the NICU equipment. My poor babies. What was it like for such tiny bags of skin to be stuffed with heavy liquid? Did their itty-bitty blood vessels soak up the fresh blood like sponges or did they burst from the pressure? I can see the Blue Baby's veins through his translucent skin. They don't look like blood vessels. They look like squiggles from a ballpoint pen.

I feel myself teetering toward a black, emotional abyss. If I don't get out of here, my heart will explode. I haven't even seen the Red Baby yet. I try to breathe, but the air feels lodged in my chest. Maybe they should have breathing machines for the parents too.

"Oh, and please tell Aunt Rita 'thank you' on behalf of the nurses." The charge nurse hands me a card.

Thank you to the doctors and nurses who are taking care of my nephews.

Love, Aunt Rita

"It came with the arrangement. The biggest edible bouquet I've ever seen. It was like this." She opens her arms wide.

It takes me a moment to connect the dots. Matt's Aunt Rita lives 2,000 miles away, and she's sent a present to people she doesn't even know—people *I* don't even know. What a strange thing to do. As far as I'm concerned, these nurses haven't proven themselves yet.

"There was pineapple and melons carved to look like flowers. It was amazing. We devoured it in minutes. Even the kale is gone," says the nurse from Red Baby's corner of the room.

Maybe it's supposed to be an incentive, like a signing bonus or tipping the maid before she cleans the room.

At the other end of the room, the Red Baby squirms in his isolette.

The Red Baby's nurse nods to me. "If you've washed your hands, you can touch him. Put one hand on his head and the other on the soles of his feet, like this." She holds her hands up like she's holding an imaginary loaf of bread.

"Don't make any strokes or light touches," she warns. "It's too over-stimulating for their nervous systems. You'll know because they'll turn their heads away or put a hand up, like they're saying, 'Stop!' " She gestures. She looks like she's one of the Supremes. *Stop! In the name of love!*

I open the little doors of the Red Baby's isolette and put one hand on his head, the other on his feet. *So you're the guy who flitted about, back and forth*, I think. His fingernails are pink and perfectly shaped, as if they are part of an exquisitely carved sculpture. He looks huge. I was expecting something I could hold in the palm of my hand. Twelve inches. Just 24 hours ago *two* 12-inch things were inside me. Kicking, rolling, avoiding the heart monitor.

You should still be a fetus. But you're not; you're a baby. I feel a swell of pride.

I don't know if he is asleep, but the Red Baby sure is moving a lot. If I squint, his movements look active and spunky. But if I am honest with myself, he looks jittery and frenetic. He doesn't look like a miracle of nature and science; he doesn't even look human. He looks like a bald kitten or like an alien—E.T. or Dr. Zaius from *Planet of the Apes*.

I hold my foot-long baby between my palms. He feels…*scared.* It's the same body language my little girl exhibits when she's scared: slightly rigid, wanting me to hold her yet pulling away from me and into herself at the same time. The Red Baby feels stiff that way.

With my daughter, I mean it when I promise, "I will make sure that nothing bad will happen to you." But I can't promise anything to my baby boys. No one—not even the experts—knows what's going to happen. All I can do is hold his head and hold his feet and cry big, sloppy tears that drop on the little plastic doors of his bed. It occurs to me that my newborn sons have gone through more in one day of life than what I've been through in 40 years. I don't know if they will be all right. It occurs to me that *I* am scared too.

The Red Baby turns his head away from me and holds his hand outstretched over his face, palm outwards. *Stop! In the name of love!*

A loud beeping startles me. One of the numbers on the monitor is flashing yellow. I jerk my hands out of the isolette as if I have been caught with my hand in the cookie jar.

The Red Baby's nurse adjusts some dials.

"This is totally normal for babies of this age," she says. "It's called a de-sat. It happens all the time. He just needs a little more oxygen. Right now he's at 50, which is high. When the number stops flashing, I'll lower it." Her voice is calm, nonchalant. I feel a twinge of shame that I have over-reacted.

"Our air is only about 19 percent oxygen. A long time ago they gave preemies air that was a 100 percent O2, not realizing that in high concentrations, it's a poison. That's why Stevie Wonder is blind. He had retinopathy of prematurity. ROP, for short. Don't worry. Your boys will get checked regularly to see if they have it. And there's a laser surgery they do nowadays to prevent blindness."

Oh my God. Too much oxygen is a poison? They're giving my babies poison? How much is too much?

Instead, I turn to Matt. "Did you hear that? Stevie Wonder was a preemie!" I flash my best fake smile. He jerks up and matches my enthusiasm.

"Whoa! That's amazing!" he exclaims, a little too loudly.

"You're in good company, sweetie!" I coo to The Red Baby.

The nurse shakes her head and presses a hand to her chest. "Oh. You're handling this so we-ell!" She stretches the word "well" into two syllables. A beeping interrupts her. It's the Blue Baby. Matt and I look at each other, frozen, panicked. But the nurses exchange smiles.

"It's a twin thing," says the Blue Baby's nurse. "That happens all the time too. One twin has a de-sat and then the other one does. It's the weirdest thing."

For so many months, I've been pretending that we were not headed for this outcome. I thought that I'd be different, that I'd be the one mono-mono twin mother to deliver healthy five-pound babies at 35 weeks. I worried that preparing for the worst-case would surreptitiously cause it to happen. Now, I'm relieved to admit that I'm scared and I don't know what to do.

I don't know yet that it will get worse before it gets better. That it will take another three weeks—after the twins' heart surgery—for the boys to go from critical to stable, and two years for them to go from stable to "normal."

But I do know that we will name the the Red Baby "Michael" after his paternal grandfather and the the Blue Baby "Wagner"—the maiden name of my mother-in-law. I know that Matt and I will come to the hospital every day, and that we will tuck our daughter into bed every night. I don't know how long this fear will last, but I know that I can't pretend that I'm not scared.

"We'll just have to be scared together, Michael," I whisper.

"Look!" Michael's nurse points to the yellow number on the monitor. "He can hear you. He knows your voice! This is the oxygen-saturation number. It's going up. That's a good sign."

Wagner's nurse looks at her monitor and nods. Wagner's numbers are going up too. Matt catches my eye, and I know we are sharing the same thought: *Must be a twin thing.*

I don't know that the boys' personality differences are already present. That they will learn the possessive pronoun "ours" before they learn the word "mine." That even when they are in kindergarten, they will sleep in identical positions. That in a few short years, no one would ever guess that they were micro-preemies. I'll learn that twin laughter is contagious. And I'll learn that being scared together is better than pretending that everything is fine.

I put my hands back in Michael's isolette. His skin feels warm. My hands feel strong. At this moment, it's hard to say who is comforting whom.

Janine Kovac was a ballet-dancer-turned-software-engineer when she discovered that her surprise pregnancy was a high-risk twin pregnancy. Her NICU-related essays have appeared in Pregnancy and Newborn *magazine,* Raising Happiness, *and in the anthologies* Mamas Write: 29 Tales of Truth, Wit, and Grit *and* Nothing But the Truth So Help Me God. *In 2012 Janine helped co-found the 501c3 nonprofit writing group Write on Mamas. She is an event producer for Litquake and the 2016 director for the San Francisco production of Listen To Your Mother. Janine lives with her husband and three children in Oakland, California.*

MAKING PEACE WITH IMPERFECT

AMY PATUREL, M.S., M.P.H.

I reached into the plastic box and my newborn son's tiny hand gripped my index finger. Weighing only four pounds, I could barely see him beneath the shock of tubes, wires, and tape. Just a few feet away, his twin brother was lying in an identical box. Almost a full pound heavier, he was sunning himself under "jaundice lights," his eyes covered with deceptively cute baby goggles.

Are these really my babies, I wondered, as a litany of dreaded possibilities raced through my mind. *What if they're not okay?*

Despite my five-page birth plan, my sons' entrance into this world wasn't the joyful experience I anticipated, starting with hospitalized bed rest at 25 weeks to manage pre-term labor. After two months staring at the same four walls, my contractions kicked into high gear. A bedside ultrasound revealed Baby A's umbilical cord blocking his entrance through the birth canal.

"These babies are coming tonight," said my doctor, holding my hand reassuringly. "If we wait any longer, we could cut off Baby A's air supply."

I was numb. After weeks of painting the ideal birth scene, complete with subdued lighting, quiet tones and immediate nursing post-delivery, my vision of holding my babies after they were born evaporated. On a conscious level, I knew the odds of a complicated birth were high, but I had been collaborating with my boys for weeks. They were both head down and in position.

We were two days shy of the developmental safety zone of 34 weeks—a critical milestone since I knew babies delivered before then typically spend their first days in the Neonatal Intensive Care Unit (NICU).

As the nurses wheeled me into the operating room, frigid air engulfed me. Instead of soothing voices lulling me into a meditative state, a team of nurses strapped me down to a table like a prison inmate awaiting execution. The fluorescent lights shone so bright it was impossible to shut them out—even with my eyes closed.

I wanted to scream, "Wait! My boys aren't ready to be born yet—and even if they are, they wouldn't want to be ripped from my body like this." Instead, I held my husband's gaze, grabbed his hand in a white-knuckled grip, and tried to breathe.

It felt like hours passed before I heard my first son's muffled cry rise above the surgical slurps, burps, slushes and suctions. Then a minute later my second son wailed—much louder than the first—almost as if to say, "Put me back in, you jerks!

Hearing my boys cry for the first time was incredible— they were breathing! But it was also bittersweet. There was no baby on my chest after birth, no skin-to-skin contact, no opportunity to whisper, "I love you" into their ears, and certainly no time to put them to my breast.

I saw both boys for only a second before nurses whisked them into a side room where a team of neonatologists aspirated their lungs, checked their heart rates, and gave them APGAR scores. I was grateful my sons were born in a hospital equipped to deal with any problems they might have. I was also devastated.

My babies couldn't hear my voice. They couldn't smell me or touch my skin. They couldn't feel my presence. I was trapped in recovery while strange faces strapped them to monitors, poked them with needles and attached them to IVs.

They were less than one minute old, and already I felt like I'd left an indelible scar on their psyches. I worried they would feel abandoned, that they would miss the voice they had heard from inside the womb.

"Go with our boys," I told my husband, Brandon, trying to hold back tears.

He grasped my hand, "I don't want to leave you."

"I'm fine; they're all alone. I want them to hear a familiar voice." I pleaded.

Four hours later a transporter finally wheeled me down to the NICU on a gurney. I couldn't touch my babies from my bed-on-wheels, but I could peer over the side railing. I barely got a glimpse of my little guys before our three-minute supervised visit ended.

I watched helplessly as the nurses in the NICU tried to mechanize the human processes I had been providing for my babies. In an instant, they became their primary caregivers—not me and Brandon. I wasn't the first, the second or even the third person to hold them. I felt cheated. Guilty. Like I was already failing as a mom. I couldn't keep my boys safe. I couldn't soothe them when they cried. Those duties fell to others more qualified than me.

The following four days were a mix of agony and pain, with a few magical moments connecting with my sons. Recovery from the C-section was especially difficult because I had been confined to a bed for weeks. All of my operating systems ground to a halt so my body could focus on protecting and nourishing my babies. My resting heart rate dropped, my lung capacity decreased, even my bowels slowed to a point where the unmentionables were impossibilities, and that caused excruciating pain.

"You can't go to the NICU until you can walk to the bathroom," said the nurse, before explaining that if I wanted to feel better and relieve the trapped gas, I had to walk.

Yeah, right, I thought. *I can't even sit on the edge of my bed without feeling woozy. How am I going to walk seven feet to the toilet?*

I couldn't tell whether the pain was from surgery, bed rest, bowel issues or a combination of all three. But the result was the same: I couldn't see my babies!

Brandon felt guilty. "It's not fair that I can see them and you can't."

"You're right; it's not fair," I replied. "But I need you to hold our guys as much as possible."

I knew premature babies needed holding. I knew skin-to-skin contact with a parent helped them regulate their breathing, maintain their body temperature, even gain weight. They'd have to achieve all three before they could be discharged. I knew if I couldn't be there, Brandon was the best stand-in. They knew his voice, too.

Almost 40 excruciating hours had passed before I got clearance to see my babies. Giddy with anticipation, I brushed my teeth, combed my hair, even dabbed on some sweet-smelling, phthalate-free lotion, no small feat considering that getting up to pee required Herculean effort. I was doped up on narcotics for the shooting pains in my abdomen. It felt like tiny knives constantly stabbing me from the inside out. But all I cared about was getting closer to my boys.

When I scrubbed in outside the NICU, I learned I couldn't hold them without asking a nurse first. I looked around the room and quickly discovered our sons didn't even have the comfort of each other. Packed together in the womb like sardines, they were more connected to each other than to me. Each feeling the other's kicks, somersaults, and hiccups. Now, they were completely isolated in industrial strength plastic boxes, separated by a few feet with foreign noises blaring at them 24 hours a day.

"How can they sleep with all that racket?" I asked while other newborns screamed and cried above the beeps, alarms, and loud voices.

"They're used to noise," the nurse replied. "It's loud inside the womb."

The nurses' expertise and intricate monitoring machines silenced my maternal instincts. Fear overwhelmed me.

They're so small! What if I hold them wrong? What if they choke while I'm trying to feed them? What if I over-stimulate them?

"I'm wildly unprepared to take care of them," I lamented to my husband.

"You'll be great," he said, reassuringly.

With the nurses' help, I learned to diaper, bathe, feed and soothe my babies amidst their medical paraphernalia. I also learned that just being there, holding them close, was the most comfort I could offer all four of us.

For the next 19 days, I traveled back and forth to the hospital, an hour each way. I took a receiving blanket from each of my sons every night, burying my nose in their scent, and called every morning, waiting with a pounding heart as I asked the nurse for a progress report on their feeding, breathing and body temperature.

When they jumped through the required hoops and got their discharge papers, I still didn't feel like their mom. But as we strapped our boys into their car seats and prepared for the drive home, I knew Brandon and I were gaining control of our family life.

Even though their first days weren't ideal, I've realized pigeonholing our boys into my world of perfectionism isn't fair. They won't remember a single moment of those 19 days. But I will. What I choose to remember, well, that's up to me.

Each day when Brandon and I dance with our sons in our living room and watch their faces light up as they giggle with delight, I realize how unimportant the imperfect days are. Can I say that I've come to terms with my babies' premature birth? No, but my outlook on life is different because of it. The whole harrowing ordeal shaped who we are as a family. It shaped who they are. And they are perfect.

Amy Paturel is an award-winning writer who has chronicled her triumphs, heartbreaks and parenting escapades for Parents, Fit Pregnancy, American Baby, *the* New York Times *and* Newsweek. *When she's not trying to master the art of raising three boys without losing her mind, she teaches essay writing and pens service stories about health, fitness, food and wellness for consumer and custom magazines. Amy lives in a bleary-eyed fog, populated by giant LEGO towers, remote control cars, and captivating renditions of "The Hot Dog Dance."*

SAME TIME LAST YEAR

LEXI ROHNER

I have missed whole seasons. Time has passed, and suddenly it is 108 degrees outside. Many months past were spent singeing our nasal lining with the stench of hospital air. The pregnancy and birth of our premature triplets was a birth of our own, and I realized that this time last year we were only hoping to get pregnant.

The latter part of my pregnancy was spent beached alternately in a hospital bed or a living room recliner, affording precious thinking time. We believe we are different than animals. We have cars, make-up, jobs, coffee, books. Everything my body demanded of me, every eating desire, sleeping manner, is primal. Nature was preparing me to care for my children. Humbling.

When my water broke, I was simply terrified of having babies that night. Three years of fertility treatments puncturing my skin, invading my guts, quarter-sized bruises that made chicken pox scars jealous and unwavering optimism had not prepared me for this. Paralyzed by my drenched legs at 11 PM, I haphazardly grabbed 'necessities' when we decided it was time to go to the hospital. Was I going to care about lip balm? I was not ready. Arriving at the Emergency Room 30 minutes later, frenzy erupted and whirred past my overloaded horizontal body when the nurses discovered I was already ten centimeters dilated and could have given birth in the car.

I was petrified we would lose our babies, or I would die, leaving my husband with three newborns. Fourteen holes in my back attempting to administer a spinal block rendered me immobile, feeding my hideous claustrophobia. A new empathy for the disabled washed over me as I willed my uncooperative limbs to move. The irony of this experience would not fully envelop me for months. Two hours later, I was a mother to 28-week premature triplets.

The first week was the most difficult of our lives. Both of our boys suffered pulmonary hemorrhages, and one had a severe stroke, necessitating a move to a larger hospital. It was excruciating to witness his medical complications, and I cried out at night for missing him. They asked if we wanted to take him off life support. "Your baby is brain damaged. Would you like to kill him?" is what I heard. My insides were mush and my whole being irrevocably damaged as I stoically peered back at the neonatologist. A wave of sympathy for the doctor suddenly washed over me in the midst of his delivery of such horrific news and impossible choices. I only had to hear this once. He had to utter these kinds of words every day. The extent of our son's damage and his laundry list of issues would be unknown for years. But this little boy was ours, and we could not let him go. I just knew in my heart he would be okay.

Before their birth, we had no knowledge of prematurity, disabilities, therapeutic services, IEPs, and many other acronyms we would come to learn. Under three pounds each and smaller than the palm of my hand, they slipped into this world with a myriad of struggles ahead. A most beautiful sound was our daughter's creaky little voice when her ventilator tube was finally out. I could not swallow when I tried to grasp that my babies lived in the NICU. I had no idea when they would come home. I pushed away the thought that maybe they would not.

When I was released a few days later, nothing had changed, yet everything had. I left my home happy and hopeful (and huge). Pain smacked me full force as I returned with no babies in my hands, no babies in my belly, stepping into a house full of shower decorations, moving boxes and a confused, yearning heart. Silence near their NICU isolettes was required when visiting, lest we disturb the delicate life inside. Not being allowed to hold them for almost a week nearly killed me. I could never have imagined 'visiting' my babies. I called the nurses at all hours to inquire about their condition, feeling desperate in the black of my mind and the dark of the night.

I never expected parenting would be easy. I only expected babies. What we had before us now was beyond my comprehension. What if they had been born in perfect condition? That would not exempt them from some other harm later in life. It is all a roll of the dice. I would worry just the same. Crying would be a daily occurrence. Waterproof mascara would have been a joke and a waste of time. I trekked daily to two hospitals, holding each baby as often and as long as I could.

Touching them was an undeniable sedative. What small creatures to have such power over my heart.

Same Time Five Years Later

"Mama, he hit me!"

"Stop bothering her and talking so much, PLEASE!" I hear myself say loudly.

I laugh, realizing I just told my brain-damaged child to stop talking and bothering his sister. Wait, the kid who just began walking at nearly five years old is pestering YOU?? It is a freaking miracle. Thirteen brain surgeries, two VP shunts, one eye surgery, a parade of therapists in and out of our house for years and grieving over 'what could have been'. For a moment, life feels normal.

Parents are proud when their child achieves something. We all want happiness for our children. Then, there is the moment you experience happiness you could not have anticipated when you are forced to divest yourself of the expectations you had for life as a parent. It is the moment your child does something that defies what doctors and professionals said they might not do. Like live.

Lexi Rohner wrote her first book at age seven and won a library summer contest for reading the most books. Her FAQ about life with loud, messy and expensive 7-year-old triplets (two with special needs), an 18-year-old stepson and her children's 11 grandparents offers one answer: don't fold anything. A lifelong competitive figure skater, Rohner left her 13-year hospitality management career to coach skating for 11 years. Rohner created a monthly column for SKATING Magazine and found her previous experience in voiceover and as a camp director oddly handy for the unexpected adventures of parenting multiples.

LUCKY

ERIKA SIGURDSON

Two days after my twins were born, the sky over Reykjavik turned the strangest color. The enormous windows of the NICU looked out to Hallgrimskirkja, the city's most iconic landmark, flanked by summer-green birches. But on that day, all was suffused with this weird, unnatural light, roiling gray clouds lit up in electric orange. Inside the hospital, my babies were being treated for jaundice. Their two incubators glowed a shocking blue, the blue of tropical Kool-Aid and tanning beds. Sitting back in my black leather armchair, I wondered at the surreal contrast: electric blue against electric orange. It was the same city I had lived in for two years, and yet somehow completely unrecognizable.

Early in our time in Iceland's only NICU, I became convinced that the baby across the way from us was going to die. His monitors went off constantly. Nurses scrambled around him with outsized needles, gauze, strange medical implements. Our first day there our nurse, Hófy, explained the rules of NICU: wash your hands, stay home if you are sick, give the other parents their privacy.

"It was the way she said it," I told my husband. "'Give them their privacy.' She was talking about that baby; I just know it."

The baby went home on a Friday, his mother beaming as she invited us to see him, dressed to leave the hospital. I was thankful, embarrassed, and happy for her. Yet what I remembered after she left was the sight of surgeons surrounding the cot, and my sick certainty that something was horribly wrong.

My twins were born at 30 weeks, rushed from the delivery room to their incubators in the NICU. Earlier in the pregnancy, they had been diagnosed with TTTS—twin to twin transfusion syndrome, an imbalance of the blood vessels connecting the babies and the placenta. They were shocking colors at birth: Florence, anemic-pale, and Olivia, an unnatural iron-rusty red.

The first night after they were born, I slept more soundly than I had in months. In those first mornings after their birth, I felt no new-parent anxiety, no driving need to check their breathing or adjust their blankets. Of course they were breathing, with monitors and nurses to watch over them. But in the absence of normal new-parent anxiety, instead we had strange, unexpected fears to keep us up at night.

Our girls were so small: 2 pounds, 4 ounces and 2 pounds, 8 ounces, respectively. The hospital's smallest diapers sagged over their little bottoms and rode up to their armpits. The blue light of their jaundice treatment picked out the fine fair hairs on their backs and shoulders—the lanugo—and accentuated the color difference between them. Florence, who was smaller than her sister, had these funny, muscle-like bulges on the top of her shoulders, like biceps that needed to drop about halfway down the upper arm. She was thin and wrinkly and muscly, like a wiry old man who had been strong once.

Olivia, though bigger, struggled more. She needed breathing assistance and glucose feedings through the IV line in her navel. Most worryingly, there was a chance she was developing a blood clot in the brain.

"It is a very small possibility," our doctor said soothingly. An athletic, middle-aged man with a strong accent, his most prominent feature was his graying strawberry-blond chest hairs, pushing out of the V of his scrubs. "And it is only a

Stage 1—that is very important if you are going to Google it. Stage 1, and only a very small possibility."

I didn't Google it, though it was a struggle. I had already cried my way through images of 29-week babies, through grim descriptions of TTTS outcomes, through the fear of intrauterine laser surgery and its risks to the babies. We didn't even tell our families about the blood clot. We had already shared so much bad news, so much uncertainty.

That afternoon, still worrying about the clot, I visited the babies on my own. I walked into tumult; nurses huddled around Olivia's incubator, all white uniforms, and practiced motion. The baby screamed while they worked. I peeked in—saw cords and hands, a small flash of blood. I drew back, feeling for the first time unwelcome, out of place. Olivia kept screaming and I ducked around a corner, tears coming hard.

It was over quickly. It was good news. Olivia was strong enough to have the navel IV removed, leaving only her CPAP for breathing, and cords to monitor her heart and lungs. After that, she did as well as her sister—sometimes better, as she continued to be the bigger baby.

Like so many of our pregnancy fears, the clot faded slowly, not resolved in some grand moment. Olivia grew stronger as the days went by. She came off her CPAP only a day after Florence. Her digestion worked; she breathed soundly. By the time her MRI pronounced her fine two weeks later, it was almost an afterthought.

In those early days, it felt like the pregnancy simply continued without me. The babies slept and stretched inside their incubators in much the same way that they slept and stretched inside me. They curled their fingers in a soft, fluid motion that I remembered as tickles in my side. They would lay still, then suddenly jerk their legs out in these intense, sharp kicks that in utero would ripple on the surface of my belly.

Our first weekend, the twins were alone in H-1, the highest intensity ward. The nurse in charge of them that weekend was Gudrun, a Valkyrie-tall woman in her early thirties, kind and straightforward with just the tiniest suggestion of a younger, gawkier self. Gudrun made me ecstatically happy by telling us, just off-hand, that the twins were perfectly well enough to move to H-2.

"If there was an emergency, we'd move them," she said, shrugging her majestic shoulders. "You might as well stay here for now. More privacy." She waved at the empty ward. "No emergencies now."

Gudrun showed us how to prepare milk for the babies' feedings, guiding my burly, bearded husband as he learned to put on tight blue rubber gloves and a flimsy plastic apron, and carefully weigh out 0.5 ounces of pumped breast milk for the two o'clock feed. She showed us how to change diapers around wires and tubes, maneuvering awkwardly through the small holes in the incubators. Most excitingly, Gudrun encouraged me to do kangaroo care with both babies at once, something I had wanted to do since they were born but dared not ask. When she pulled them out of their incubators, they seemed so tiny and frail; I almost changed my mind. But when she placed them on my chest, somehow they didn't seem so small. They were hot and soft and smelled like new babies, and if I twisted my head in just the right way, I could bend down and kiss the tops of both of their heads.

Florence spent almost two hours with her face buried in between my breasts, pushing her sister Olivia off to one side. She burrowed herself in so deep I worried that she couldn't breathe—but, of course, the monitor showed she was fine. Still, I had to poke and tickle her every few minutes to see her twitch and burrow deeper, just to feel safe. After a long while, she moved into a different position, so that I held both babies cradled in my arms, with Florence curled up around my right nipple. Her breathing monitor, which was glued to her chest, ended up on my areola, confusing the readings. Although I could barely breathe, I didn't want it to ever end.

In those moments, we felt almost normal. There was always the fear hanging over us, that something might go wrong, that the girls were doing too well, that it couldn't last. The worst days were ones when on the way into NICU, we passed surgical teams in their mint-greens. I would continue with my hand washing, the smell of the alcohol burning my nose, turning to acid fear in my stomach. I wouldn't breathe right until I pushed through the doors, turning the corners to reach my babies, sleeping unawares in their little twin bassinet. Other days as we entered the NICU, we would pass women crying on the couch at the entrance of the unit, or staring hard into the distance. Seeing them, we would lower our voices, quiet our laughter. There were always doctors in mint-greens on those days.

Time passes so strangely in the NICU. Every day is the same: the same rituals, the same duties. In the long, Icelandic summer days, we hardly noticed the afternoons passing to evening, until Ulla, the evening nurse, arrived, and our stomachs told us it was time to go home. We knew it was the weekend only because the nurses did 12-hour shifts instead of eight.

My favorite time of year in Iceland is when the lupine is in bloom, sometime in early July—huge, open swathes of blue lighting up the moorlands around Reykjavik. We missed it completely that year, never even noticed. For six weeks all we saw was the walk from our house to the hospital. We memorized the details: the frozen yogurt shop that marked the halfway point, the exotic fish aquarium in the lobby of the children's hospital, the creaky elevators up to the third-floor NICU.

My husband grumbled, "I'm so sick of this walk!" He would try to work out how many times he had done it. "Twice a day for five weeks, except for that one Tuesday..."

Slowly but surely, our babies got ready to leave. They started feeding on their own, impossibly small amounts at first, then more and more. One day, Florence weighed in at 4 pounds, 4 ounces—the magic number for leaving the NICU. The chatty, dark-haired midwife, Margret, told us that afternoon.

"We were so happy, weren't we, Florence? We did a victory dance all around the room! *Sigurdans*, victory dance!"

We started interacting more with the other parents. One mother helped me move the twins and told me with a tired smile that she might finally go home that weekend. A new couple moved into her spot; the father talked soccer with my husband, and we exchanged knowing smiles over the difficulties of feeding, changing, and maneuvering around the long monitor cords.

Then, just like that, they were ready to go home. We spent two nights in the hospital, getting used to the idea of being alone with the babies. Then we left. A quick physical exam, a rush of goodbyes. The NICU was getting ready for triplets, expected by C-section that afternoon. Our spot had already been repurposed; the small space rearranged to make room for the new arrivals. We felt a little like bandits, making off with our babies—but we were free to leave.

A few days after the girls came home, I found myself walking the same route one last time—back from the pharmacy, next to the hospital. Just a few minutes away, I passed a house on the corner of our back lane: gray concrete with heavy, square windows, a bright red door, and a small garden shed in the same color. Yellow poppies had bloomed and gone to seed in the cracks between the pavement and the garden wall. The weather was pleasant for Iceland: clear, still, and almost warm. The neighborhood cats were out, rolling on the sun-warmed pavement. From inside the red garden shed, a band played—gentle, airy electronica, in a typically Icelandic style. I stopped, briefly, enjoying the music and the late-summer warmth. After a short moment, I pushed on, taking the last few steps towards home, and my napping babies.

Erika Sigurdson is a writer, historian, and mother of identical twin girls. An expert in medieval Iceland, she has recently moved home to Canada after a two-year fellowship in Reykjavik. Her twins born in June 2015, keep her busy.

JOURNAL IT

_____

Write your thoughts and feelings down. Capture the moments. Life with multiples is exciting and busy, and it's easy to forget the little things and details. Here are some writing prompts to help you along.

The NICU is always the best place for babies who need medical care, especially if they are premature—as many multiples tend to be. Find ways to stay positive. Write down what makes you feel positive about life right now.

What beautiful moments did you have with your multiples while in the NICU?

THE FIRST YEARS

BREASTFEEDING MULTIPLES —IT'S POSSIBLE!

ALISON LEE

Many mothers, especially first-timers, want to breastfeed their babies. What if you're expecting multiples? The very idea is daunting, even for a seasoned parent. I had already successfully breastfed two children for 18 months and 22 months respectively, yet I still felt intimidated by the idea, knowing with certainty that breastfeeding is a commitment on all fronts—physically, emotionally, and mentally.

If you do anything at all, do this first: arm yourself with knowledge, even if your multiples are not your first babies. The best research is talking to other moms of multiples who have breastfed their children, and there are many books and websites at your disposal (refer to our Multiples Resources page for more information).

Here are my best tips from someone who's been there, done that (at the time of writing, I am still breastfeeding my 16-month-old twins).

- Begin breastfeeding as soon as you're able. If your babies end up in the NICU, a breast pump is essential to keep up your milk supply. I couldn't breastfeed my twins until they were a few days old, but I pumped daily. Premature babies *can* breastfeed. You just need patience.

- When they're bigger and out of NICU, feed your babies at the same time. Tandem feeding sounds tricky, and can be in the beginning, but you'll get used to it quickly. A twin-nursing pillow is your best friend. There are various ways you can position the babies—try them all, and do what works best for you.

- Ask for help! Your spouse can help move the babies on and off the nursing pillow, or bring you water and snacks. If you have issues with latching or milk supply, or need the support and assurance that you're doing well, ask a lactation consultant for advice.

- To keep up milk supply, feed often and pump when you can.

- If you have more than two babies, manage your expectations. Keeping up a milk supply for twins is doable, but to do so for three or more babies is hard work. It is possible, but know that it's okay if you can't manage. Consider supplementing with formula and bottles. There is no shame in that.

- Breastfeeding any number of babies is hard work and a lot to ask of your body. Look after yourself. Eat well, rest, and stay hydrated.

- Keep track of your babies' feeds (who fed for how long on which breast, and when) with smartphone apps such as latchMe, Babyfeeding Central, and Baby Connect.

- Moms of multiples who breastfeed are prone to issues such as milk blisters (painful white spots on the nipples), plugged ducts and mastitis. Even if you have the best practices, and your babies have no problems latching, these issues are common. One of the best websites, also recommended by Heather Conway, a lactation consultant, is kellymom.com.

• Don't expect your multiples to be the same—their feeding needs could be different, and that's okay. This is especially true as they get older.

• Breastfeed for as long as you feel comfortable, though I recommend going for at least six months. However, if you run into various problems—poor milk supply, ongoing latching issues, or health complications for both you and your babies—know that it's okay to stop.

Breastfeeding is a personal choice. Whether you do it or not, and for how long, is entirely up to you. Do what's best for your family. If you do choose to breastfeed, get support and help from your healthcare providers, family, and friends. Good luck!

ALL THINGS, ALL AT ONCE

MELANIE SWEENEY

At night, the babies do not have names. We identify them in proximity to ourselves. My baby, your baby. This baby, that baby. Is your baby asleep? This baby is hungry. Our parenting strategy is man-to-man defense. Our strategy is to divide and conquer, conquer being a relative term.

When they cry, my husband and I flee to opposite ends of the house. We try to discern when we pick which baby to hold, who might quiet the easiest, sleep the fastest. Like Russian roulette with infants. When the house quiets, we shuffle on our little circuit (bedroom to hall, hall to living room), passing silently like ships in the night, shushing our tiny sleeping cargo.

This early stage of parenting twins is lonely. We are always apart, it seems, and always with a baby.

From the start of our marriage, Josh and I tended to do the big things together, at the same time. Our wedding was on a Friday, we moved out of state Saturday morning, and we reported to graduate school and our new jobs that Monday. Upon graduating from our MFA program, we moved out of state again, during my third trimester with our first baby. Josh missed a phone call during my labor with Theo—an offer of the job he ultimately took, relieved to start bringing in money after a summer without employment. In addition to all this, I was supposed to start a Ph.D. program two weeks after the birth (I didn't).

151

There is a short story collection by Lee K. Abbott called *All Things, All at Once.* I joked when I read it that it should be our family motto.

My mother used to say, "Don't have more kids than you have hands."

Or maybe it wasn't so prescriptive. Maybe what she had said was, "I never had more kids than hands." Whatever the exact wording, I preserved this idea in the back of my mind. I only ever wanted two children.

When I had a sonogram 12 weeks into my second pregnancy because I measured a month ahead, I immediately spotted two little black sacs and two little bouncing blobs inside them, and I said, "What am I supposed to do with two babies and a toddler?" I didn't have three hands.

Theo's infancy was a challenge. He cried a lot. He slept in short, infrequent spurts. There was a minor health scare, breastfeeding problems, the general feeling that our puzzle of a life had been scattered, a few pieces gone missing under the rug. Josh and I tag-teamed, passing his tense little screaming body back and forth—to me to nurse, to Josh to walk—but when he finally fell asleep, we met back in the living room to hug, to sigh, to say, "Good job. I love you." We marveled together at his peaceful face. "He's nice like this." A piece, sliding back into place.

There is no passing off the crying baby when they are both the crying baby. We can trade them if one seems easier to handle than the other, but this is no guarantee. If his baby calms down first, Josh will text me from the hall to propose swapping, careful to prevent the louder baby from setting the quieter one off again. *Leave her on the couch. I'll leave this one on the bed.* Then we pass by quickly, flashing a look that says, *Good luck.* That baby is pissed. Success, with twins, means we stay in separate, silent spaces, alone but keeping the peace for each other. Success means we celebrate our hard-won victories of soothing a baby, by ourselves, mentally, as we shuffle-bounce-step through the darkness.

We have each muttered, more than once, "I don't like our babies." This is us connecting.

During the day, when I am alone with all three kids, I revert to a zone defense. I run triage, mentally attaching red or yellow tags to them to sort out who needs me most. The girls, Caroline and Emerson, are almost always red. They live on me, either nursing in my lap or cuddled to my chest in the twin carrier. In a pinch, I can scoop them into my arms, one under both butts, one behind both bobbling heads. Sometimes I alternate holding them in two-minute intervals, bouncing on an exercise ball with one while I steady a pacifier in the other's mouth. "Girls," I plead. "Girls, girls, girls." Theo knows that we sing to calm the babies, so he jumps in with "The Alphabet Song" or "Twinkle Twinkle Little Star," trying to help. Except he's kind of tone deaf, and he mainly just shouts the words over their cries (Sometimes, his song of choice is "Uptown Funk," and he howls, "Uptown funk you uuuuuuup!" until quiet is restored). Still, this is preferable to when the noise overwhelms him, and he joins in with an ear-splitting, drawn-out scream. On the other side of a crying jag, I look at all of the kids and sigh. "Are you okay?" Theo asks. "Yes. Are you okay?"

When I was a new parent and had only one baby, I still felt overwhelmed most of the time. For me, motherhood was a process of splitting and separating, even as, in some ways, I became fuller, more focused, better defined. To put things in perspective, I told myself, "At least I don't have twins." I know better now than to say, "At least I don't have triplets."

Between the three of my children, I am always weighing how often I've made eye contact with them, how long I've held them, how much of me they've gotten. No matter the breakdown, I am always lacking, but we get through the day anyway. Another mom of multiples told me once that being fair doesn't always mean giving equal portions of everything. I remember this when Theo is watching his second hour of TV while Emerson is eyeing me from her swing and Caroline is nestled to my chest. Later, I'll run around outside with Theo. Emerson will get extra cuddles when she takes twice as long to nurse.

The girls had a short NICU stay following their births—four and eight days. Sometime during the few days that Caroline was home, but Emerson was not, a representative from the hospital called to check on us. I'll never forget what she said when I told her we were just eager to have both girls home, together, "Enjoy your first twin now. It'll be so much worse when you have them both there." As a parent with a baby in what felt like a hostage situation, I couldn't believe someone could utter such a stupid thing.

I know what she meant, of course. Our twins are older now, and we still struggle to coordinate outings, bedtime, baths for all three kids, though we've come a long way from the first time I tried to shove both babies into one Moby wrap for a quick walk. It ended with all of us sweaty and Caroline trying to nurse on Emerson's face.

Even when they were both in the NICU, we had at least two of our three children in the same place. They were stationed on opposite sides of the room, so Josh and I had to either stay together and visit them one at a time, leaving the other alone, or we had to split up and each sit with one baby for an hour, then switch. Mostly, we wanted both babies to be with someone for longer, so we separated. For long, lonely stretches, I held one baby in my arms and hummed every song I knew, occasionally peering across at my husband doing the same thing. When I was with one, I was without the other. This need to be in two (or three) places at once, this ache, it started there.

I'd imagined my babies, hours after their birth, swaddled like burritos in the same bedside bassinet. I'd pictured them both on my chest, holding hands while they nursed. But they were attached to monitors, and their wires could stretch only a few feet. I didn't hold my babies together until Caroline left the NICU, and with a flurry of wings in my chest, I rushed her to her sister's station, and I cradled them together in my arms, desperate for a kind of magic to happen. I didn't get pictures of a double baby bassinet. I didn't get to dress them in the little coordinating sleepers I'd packed in their untouched baby bag. But that reunion of the three of us, finally, was every bit as important as the images I'd hoped to slip into their baby books.

The joke about having more than one child is that you learn to relax a bit with your subsequent child, maybe leaving them with a sitter sooner or failing to record every little milestone. With my twins, I find myself caring more about my milestones than when they rolled over for the first time. My first time tandem baby-wearing successfully in public. My first time tandem breastfeeding. When I accomplish a new twin parenting skill, I share pictures and tell everyone I know.

On the other hand, there are days when I resent the extra hurdles I have to jump over just to accomplish the simplest tasks. Strangers tell me I'm awesome. They look at me wearing two babies on my chest, a toddler in tow, and they say, "You're Supermom." Sometimes, I just want to be a regular mom. It does feel, sometimes, like I need a third hand, a roll of duct tape, and another Master's degree just to get through a day.

Something as simple as a trip to Target to break up a long, stressful day at home is a gamble. Will they cry the whole way there? Will Theo refuse to leave the Hot Wheels aisle when I have both babies on my chest and I can't lift him into the cart for a quick getaway?

When the babies were two months old, I was suffocating at home. The crying was getting louder, the walls closer, somehow, and summer in Texas meant we couldn't just pop out for a walk. It took an hour to leave: feed the babies, clothe them, get the toddler to put on pants, strap everyone into their various seats in the van. One was crying as I parked at Target, so I thought, I'll just let her nurse for a minute. Soon after she latched on, the other baby started to fall apart. I was trapped by their car seats in the center of the van and couldn't climb back into the front and out the door while holding a baby; I knew she'd cry again if I put her back in her seat. I was desperate to limit the crying to one baby in such a tight, enclosed space. I ended up with one in the front seat, one in the way back, and me in the middle trying to strap on the twin carrier to get them inside the store. Knowing I couldn't reach back to unbuckle Theo's car seat once the bulk of both babies was on my chest, I went ahead and let him out. So, there I was, with the girls on opposite ends of the van and screaming, and I was hunched over and wedged in the middle, trying to figure out the carrier. That's when Theo snaked around me to the front and immediately began pushing buttons, shouting, "A! B! C! D!" and bumping the heat up to 85 degrees.

I froze for about 10 seconds, disbelieving, afraid there was no way out of this—all the kids were at or approaching red, and so was I—and I looked out the side window. The panic lifted as quickly as it came. I saw myself as a random passerby might, hearing the screams from inside a van and peeking in at a sweaty, panting, unwashed mother, half-strangled by baby carrier fabric. I laughed. I laughed so hard my chest opened back up. Then I slipped my crying babies into the carrier, moved a car seat to unblock our exit, took my son's hand, and emerged from the van into the sunlight like the slow hero montage of a movie.

That was a defining moment for me as a mother of multiples, because it was the first time that the chaos was too much and the first time I found the whole thing hilarious instead of terrifying. I couldn't give up. We had to go to the store, or we had to get back into car seats and go home. Neither option was easy. So I took it one child at a time, step by step, and I learned that I was capable, even in the most stressful circumstances, of finding a way through.

As much as I wonder why on earth the Universe saw fit to give me twins—me, the introvert, the mom who barely managed one baby—I have to laugh sometimes at how typical this is for my family. We were cautious when we decided to try for a second child; getting two at once was surely some cosmic joke. But we do the big things all at once. Twins shouldn't have surprised us as much as it did.

Whether all my kids are pulling me in different directions, or I am trying to hold them all in my arms, close to my chest, *All Things, All at Once* reminds me that it's going to be okay. I am always splitting my attention, multitasking: tandem feeding, tandem baby-wearing, reading to my son while this baby or that baby or both sleep on me. My emotions are almost always seemingly in direct conflict— loving all my children as I sometimes resent having two of them together. Missing my husband while we each take a baby, but also appreciating and respecting him more, taking some heart in the knowledge that he's just on the other side of the same house. I miss my relationship with my son; I love how he has opened up his world to his sisters. My body feels broken by the labor of mothering multiples and an older child, but my arms are stronger than they've ever been.

This life is crushing at times. It is breathtaking. I am never enough. I am always just enough. There is room; I am starting to see, for all of it.

Melanie Sweeney is a writer and mother of a singleton boy and twin girls. She holds an MFA in creative writing from New Mexico State University. Birds as Leaves, her nonfiction chapbook on motherhood, nature, and the body, is available from The Lettered Streets Press' Split Volume Series, and she blogs at Micro-Affections.

THE MAIN ATTRACTION

BRITON UNDERWOOD

The local aquarium has a wonderful array of exhibits where you can view all sorts of aquatic life, from stingrays to sharks that you wouldn't see in daily life. Next to the stingray exhibit, where you could pet a stingray, a family stood in awe. No, they weren't in awe of seeing and touching a majestic animal; it was my sons who were drawing all their attention.

"Oh my God, honey! Look! Over there; they are twins!" A woman said excitedly, tapping her husband on the shoulder to get his attention.

Twins beat stingrays on the "cool things to see at the aquarium" chart.

I didn't realize during the shock of finding out I was going to be a father of multiples that my wife was also giving birth to the hottest attractions for the casual passerby to "ohhh" and "ahhh" at. In fact, when in public, the only people who don't seem to acknowledge our existence are the other families with twins. Surprise, right? Maybe after wading through countless people asking, "Twins?" we don't have the energy to jump in the air and shout "Twin life!" while hitting a mid-air high five. No, usually our eyes stay averted, gifting each other with a moment of tranquility that is quickly interrupted by the next couple seeing twins for what must be the first time, ever.

My kids are more interesting to look at than exotic aquatic life.

It wasn't just the stingrays that day. The penguins lost too. As did the beluga whale. And the seals. Even the sharks paled in comparison to the wonder of twins. Someone call The Discovery Channel and tell them they need to produce a Twin Week.

No matter how much the penguins waddled or the seals bobbed their heads, no one took notice. They were too busy looking at the extraordinary sight of twins! A real once-in-a-lifetime opportunity!

Two years into raising twins, I am used to it. I am used to the people who know someone who knew someone whose brother had twins. I am used to people's need to know which one is older or whether or not they are identical. I am used to, when I say they aren't identical, being met with, "Well they look identical to me!" That doesn't make them identical, but I am not going to explain to you the differences because, frankly, I fell prey to doing that too many times when they were newborns. No, the cereal aisle is not the proper place for a lesson in biology.

A trip to the grocery store usually has our hearts blessed four times, three oohs, two people who have to squeal the word "twins!" in a high-pitched voice and a partridge in a pear tree.

The ocean's most alluring animals don't have anything on my twins, why would the live lobsters from the seafood section of the grocery store?

Yes, my hands *are* full. They wouldn't be full if you didn't stop me from loading the groceries into the car and heading home. I am surprised people don't come to my house asking to see what the twins' natural habitat looks like. Their enclosures are spacious- yes, they have separate cribs.

What is with the whole "I knew it" thing after asking if they are twins, Sherlock? You deduced that the two who look eerily similar in age, height and appearance were twins. Spot on, but why did you feel the need to step in front of us and stop us so that you can ask a question you knew the answer to?

"Did you plan them?"

You don't plan twins. How would you do that? Yeah, my wife planned to knock it all out in one pregnancy. We wanted one of them to be a girl, but that would have taken even more planning.

"Do twins run in your family?"

Well, you can see they certainly don't walk. Excuse me while I chase down those two wonders headed towards the candy aisle.

"Were they natural?"

How about you take us out to eat before trying to talk about our private parts, pervert?

It is to be expected though. These kids are wonders of the modern world; of course people want to know all about the lady bits they came from.

I want to use their ability to attract a crowd to gain entry into places, like the aquarium, for free.

"Oh, we add to the experience. People like looking at our kids more than your walruses, so really you should pay us."

That will work. It has to!

I don't know what is worse—the people who come up and ask a million personal questions or the ones who, from afar, gaze at us and openly talk like we can't hear them. I am waiting for them to come up and just start petting my kids.

Please don't pet my children.

Briton Underwood, better known as Punk Rock Papa, is a parent above all else. When he gets sick of being at their beck and call he likes to escape to his Facebook page or site. He writes about any and everything he wants, but mainly about his twin boys and his newest addition—another boy. He also would like the world to know he has a beautiful wife, because the couch isn't that comfy.

SURVIVING THE TWINNING REACTION

ELLEN NORDBERG

The intense bonding connection between twins is called "the Twinning Reaction," by psychologists and researchers. My neighbor the dog trainer says, "Don't adopt two puppies from the same litter because they'll never obey you." Same concept.

The obstetrician did not hear the second heartbeat until 18 weeks. I was already panicking about motherhood—now there would be identical twin boys? I thanked the doctor for her attention to detail, gathered my wits, and tried to prepare myself.

I baby-proofed the house by tie-wrapping gates to every door, wall, and table, creating a giant escape-proof pen. To use his computer in the family room, my husband scaled a fence that resembled the trickiest obstacle on American Ninja Warrior. I bought four sets of sheets and blankets for each crib in case of midnight stereo pukeage, plus a front-to-back stroller, a side-by-side double jogger, and a fancy Maclaren fold up for travel. I budgeted for babysitters, bought 20 cases of Costco diapers, and created a Sign-up Genius meal chart for friends and family. I was ready.

I steeled myself for sleep deprivation and read about "twin speak", where the babies have their own language, and "mirror-image twins" with opposite features. What I didn't anticipate were the ways my identical boys would interact with each other that would make them as different from other children as St. Bernards are from Chihuahuas.

It started when they were newborns. I'd proudly mastered the "double football hold" to nurse both babies at once (a huge time saver once I'd wrangled 13 Boppy pillows and the wriggling uncooperative participants into place). The boys would become so synchronized and focused on nursing they hated to be interrupted, so I resorted to creative burping techniques. I'd yank a baby off with one hand by the back of his onesie, slap him over my shoulder, then clap him back onto the boob (I was not above using my teeth like a mother cat when necessary).

My parenting responses to their twin bond would continue to require this level of imagination and creativity.

Like when the babies were a month old, lying on a play mat together and waving all four hands in the air, they both began shrieking inconsolably. Were their diapers too tight? Did they need burping? My husband eventually surmised that they couldn't tell whose hands belonged to whom, and wondered if maybe they feared an octopus attack. They had no sense of boundaries or their own identity, so we learned to swaddle them to quiet their arms and their nervous systems.

At six months, we hung their bouncy seats in opposing doorways of the same hall. Eyes firmly locked as if preparing for a sumo match, each boy pushed off with his legs like a crazed kangaroo, rebounding higher and higher. This continued without either boy dropping his gaze or resting his legs until their mesmerized and motion sick five-year-old cousin puked on the carpet.

When we introduced solid foods to their diet, their bond won out over parenting every time. Axel would try anything, but Aidan was picky. During one dinner while Axel sat on his grandfather's lap, eagerly eating salmon from Grampa's plate, Aidan (with the vehemence of a body guard alerting the king to hemlock) shouted from the other end of the table. "Spit it out Axel! Spit it out!"

I resorted to chasing them around the back yard, shoving cheese sticks in their mouths like a baton wielding relay runner with reluctant partners.

When the boys were two and a half, my husband came through the front door and shouted, "What's with the blood?" I pulled my head out of the dryer. Sure enough there was a red trail on the carpet leading up the stairs. I sprinted to inspect the twins, now calmly seated in front of the Wiggles show upstairs. One boy had a deep cut down his arm, but shrugged at me in explanation.

My husband and I found a bloody, broken laundry basket and leaped to this conclusion: the boys had dragged each other through the house in the basket, but a section of plastic weave had given way, ripping a line down Axel's arm. Stopping the game to complain, cry, or fill me in would have been unnecessarily inconvenient.

At age three, I received a call from their preschool administrator suggesting we test their hearing. It seems they weren't following instructions, and the teachers feared it was because they might be hearing impaired. I related this to my friend, a mom of identical twin girls, who laughed with me like we were enjoying an Amy Poehler/ Tina Fey skit. We knew they weren't deaf; they were just so focused on playing with their twin that they blocked out the rest of the world most of the time.

A common scenario at both of our homes: Mom calling, then yelling, then screaming either or both twin names, and finally resorting to placing her face inches from theirs and bellowing at jet engine decibels with spittle flying. The children would finally glance up in shock that their mother was even in the house.

I took the "perfect hearing" diagnosis from the pediatrician back to the school, and attempted to set up individual play dates for the boys to shift up this bonding pattern. Mostly, I exceeded my babysitter budget instead.

Potty training proved to be a hundred times harder than expected due to tag teaming. Once again it was inconvenient to their focused playtime to interrupt for a diaper change. I'd walk into a room with a hand covering my nose and mouth and mumble, "Who's got the stinky diaper?" Without looking up, they'd point at each other. "Him," they'd say in unison.

I reached the outer limits of desperation and put M&Ms and Hot Wheels cars on the mantel as rewards for using the toilet. Just as Axel was coming around and enthusiastically earning prizes, Aidan used his influence once more, staring me down and yelling, "No Axel! No M&Ms!" And just like that, Axel was back in a Pull-Up.

I threw my hands up in defeat, stripped them, and sent them naked into the back yard, pooping and peeing like enthusiastic coyotes. The combination of potty shrubs and an extremely patient preschool teacher were the only tactics that eventually got them into big boy underwear.

While their connection causes them to ignore pain, hunger, bodily functions and mom's voice while playing, it can also spark synchronous crying. When the boys were seven, we got pulled over on the way to football. The officer sternly asked for my license and registration. Then he glanced behind me and caught four terrified eyes spouting cartoon-sized tears behind full pads and helmets, accompanied by voices wailing through face masks, "OH NO NO NO NO! Please don't take Mommy to the station!" The officer handed me back my license and walked away chuckling.

In the end, neither my army of strollers, meal chart, nor a garage full of diapers prepared me for my twins' connection and the ways it would undo me. Eventually we put them in different first grade classrooms, which made them more independent and slightly more obedient.

I am resigned that my "same litter" children may never give me their undivided attention, but the "Twinning Reaction" has its benefits. They have a close relationship.

They work well together on teams, playing baseball and basketball, and they're adventurous in the world because they always have a wingman.

I know that someday I'll be able to drop the cheese sticks, own clean carpets, have poop-free landscaping, and get a good night's sleep. I'll also have the comfort of knowing that each of my boys has a brother he would choose as his best friend, every time.

Ellen Nordberg's stories have appeared in the Chicago Tribune, The Denver Post, The Huffington Post, Scary Mommy, Errant Parent, *and numerous anthologies. She has performed her humorous twin essays in several Colorado Listen To Your Mother shows and is currently a co-producer of the Boulder show. She lives outside of Boulder where she spends much of her time rescuing her middle-school-aged twins' remote control drones off neighbors' roofs.*

THE OUTING

JARED BOND

At some point early on while raising multiples, you have a bad day. A really, really bad day. The type of day that makes you re-evaluate your whole parenting philosophy. It was only a few months into raising our triplets when we were confronted with such a day. And it was on that day's outing that we learned the essential rules of raising multiples.

Our really bad day started off innocently enough. The triplets were almost four months old. My wife Erin and I had started taking them on outings, primarily to keep our sanity by getting out of the house. Things had gone well, for the most part, and we were probably slightly overconfident in our abilities.

I had a plan: we'd drive to the next town so that I could show off my children to some of my former professors. I even figured Erin could push the triplets around in the stroller while I got some research done at the library. From a naïve point of view, it sounded like the perfect outing.

The plan fell apart early on when the chats with my professors took longer than expected. Catching up on the latest department news and sharing the joys and trials of raising triplets took a lot of time. A quick visit turned into an hour and though we didn't realize it, the kids were well past their feeding time. They started to fuss, but I still had another professor to see. Since college classes were still in session, and the noise from the babies was growing louder, I told Erin that I would meet her and the kids downstairs. I helped push the triplet stroller into the elevator for her and, wanting to keep to the plan, I returned to my conversation with one of my former thesis advisors.

Five minutes later my cell phone rang.

Five minutes.

That's all it took for a great outing to become one of the worst outings ever.

Erin was in a panic, and over the wails of children echoing through the phone's speaker, she shouted for me to get downstairs NOW!

Of course, the elevator had not returned yet, so I found the emergency staircase and ran the four flights of stairs down to the first floor.

The screams reverberating through the cinderblock-lined hallway brought me to the women's bathroom. Huffing and puffing, I headed in to find out what was going on, only to realize that for some reason I could not open the door to the ladies' room.

A lot can happen in five minutes.

Evidently it started in the elevator. Erin had squeezed herself into the elevator with the triplet stroller while carrying one of the fussy kids in a sling. During the ride down, one of the girls decided to spit out her pacifier onto the floor. When the elevator reached the first floor, she had to extricate herself and the stroller before the door crushed them. Then my wife had to rush back to retrieve the lost pacifier before the doors shut, trapping her on the inside and the other two on the outside. Though stressed, she managed to accomplish this feat.

Next, Erin decided to wash off the pacifier. Unable to leave the kids behind, she decided to take the kids and the stroller into the women's bathroom to rinse off the elevator germs.

It was a simple plan. But that one action would change the course of this outing, and of our future excursions.

The entrance to the women's bathroom consisted of two doors with five feet between them. We had what was called the "Triple Decker" stroller—a long stroller with three car seats stacked in a row, one behind the other. Erin had managed to maneuver the bulky stroller past the first bathroom door, but couldn't get the second door open. Wearing one child in the sling, she found herself trapped behind the stroller carrying the other two children, and was incapable of reaching the next door. She was stuck. The stroller was wedged diagonally, with the wheels preventing either door from opening. Trapped in this echo chamber, all three kids started crying.

This was where I found them. I was met at the door by a professor I didn't know. She had come out of her classroom to find the source of the ruckus. She assisted me in figuring out the problem. Prying the door open enough to slide in, I reached my wife and children. Erin was at the edge of her sanity while she tried to rock the stroller back and forth (in the few inches of space she had) in a futile attempt to calm the kids. With the professor's help, we pulled and pried on the stroller and the door until my wife could finally back out the way she had come in.

Erin was *done*. Exhausted. She gave me the look that told me we weren't going to be trying this again for a long while. Looking at the clock, we realized that we were well past the kids' feeding time, and decided to call it a day.

At that point, a wide-eyed undergraduate meekly came out of the women's bathroom, where she had been trapped for the past 15 minutes, listening to all of the chaos. "Gosh, those babies sure are loud!" she commented, as she hurried past us to her next class and away from the triplets as quickly as possible.

It was then that we decided that maybe colleges should look into having families of multiples walk around campus, as a way of providing passive birth control for the undergraduate population.

As for us, it was the first step to learning the essential rules of raising multiples. Always be willing to abandon an outing or a plan. Feed the babies on schedule. Focus on the victories rather than on the catastrophes. This time, we survived. It would, however, be another few months until we attempted an outing this big on our own again.

Before becoming a middle school English teacher, Jared Bond was a stay-at-home dad to triplets. While he doesn't remember much about that first year, he took copious notes so that he could share the experience with other parents of multiples (and himself, once he caught up on sleep).

TWIN SPEAK

_____

ANGIE KINGHORN

Late summer sun streamed through the kitchen windows. By the sink, the kale was a green ruffled bouquet, and the bowl of lemons made my mouth water in anticipation. The twins would want to help with this.

"Anne! Grant! Come on down here if you want to help with the kale chips!"

Silence. I listened for the sounds of the household but heard only creaks and sighs as the house and I breathed together.

"Y'all, come on! It's time to make kale chips!"

After eight years of mothering, silence set off alarm bells sufficient to send me up the stairs two at a time. Grant's room was empty, and at first I didn't see anyone in Anne's room either, but then I heard a giggle. Where were they? I opened the closet door but found only a rack of dresses and the mournful stare of a large stuffed manatee.

Another giggle. I looked again and saw a lump protruding from the bed skirt. Rounding the corner, I saw Grant's lower half sticking out from under the bed. He was on his tummy, legs crossed at the ankles.

"Okay, Grant. Your turn."

I blinked, realizing that Anne must be there, too, secreted completely under the bed. Phrases of conversation drifted up from under the mattress, and I strained to catch them, aware all the while that I was an outsider. This was not

173

meant for me. Not for the first time, I felt like a trespasser on private ground, a visitor to a secret garden where I will never have the key.

"Close" isn't an accurate word to describe the relationship between these two. They are two halves of one whole, distinct and separate when they need to be, yet utterly inseparable when they have a choice. And though they no longer use cryptophasia (what doctors call twin speak), having long since transitioned to English, they still understand each other so well and so exclusively that I have to categorize their communication as a secret language.

There was a time, I still remember with a shiver, when we worried they would spend their lives mute outside their twosome. At 18 months, they weren't talking, except to each other.

"Bumble bee, bumble bye, bumble round in the blue blue sky, bumble bee, bumble bye, keep away from me!"

With each "b" sound, Peggy, the speech therapist, tapped her lower lip with her index finger, leaning close to my 18-month old son. Grant stared, eyes round and huge, as she continued to sing, making exaggerated movements with her lips, carefully enunciating each syllable.

"I re-mem-ber what you did when you first came to town! You crawled up-on my arm and then ouch! when you sat down! Bumble bee, bumble bye, bumble round in the blue blue sky, bumble bee, bumble bye, keep away from me!"

She shook her finger in playful admonition on the last phrase, and Grant grinned and clapped. I smiled too and struggled to hold onto Anne.

"Oow joia noa wan noolee anan nanan!" she shrieked, the blocks I was waving in front of her forgotten. "Anan nanan!"

Immediately, Grant turned in his Bumbo seat, all interest in Peggy lost. "Weu ua paca?" he said.

Peggy's bright smile didn't waver. "Okay, Angie, I think you're going to have to take her upstairs while I work with him. If they continue with twin-speak during our sessions, they won't be able to get anything out of them."

I carried an enraged Anne upstairs and spent the next half hour trying to tempt her with toys while she shrieked incomprehensible syllables at me, tears of frustration welling in both her eyes and mine. At the end of Grant's session we switched, and Anne babbled at Peggy while Grant raged at me upstairs, determined to get past me to his sister.

Twin speak, when twins develop their private language, is intriguing in the abstract, but our experience was one of frustration. None of the other twin sets I knew developed twin speak. It sounds exciting and mysterious, playing into the sci-fi notion that many people hold about the almost psychic powers of twins. When I first heard about it, I envisioned something like pig Latin: private, cute, but ultimately decipherable.

The reality was neither cute nor decipherable. Having a language of their own meant that they failed to develop their ability to speak English on a normal schedule. They hit 18 months of age and weren't talking. For all we could tell, the babies were able to understand our language as much as any child their age could, but they had no interest in speaking it back to us. My friends with singletons kept running lists of the new words their toddlers learned, and mine showed absolutely no interest in talking to anyone except each other. They shared a room, and when I listened to the baby monitor it sounded like they were having deep, philosophical conversations—in Martian.

It took us some time to realize what we assumed was a continuation of baby sounds, had evolved. Babble turned to first words, and then sentences in their language instead of ours. The odd syllables had a familiar conversational cadence, a rhythm that made sense if you listened with your fingers stuffed in your ears. Questions rose, and exclamations fell. They were communicating. Time after time I watched as my children talked to each other in this strange language of their making, using it to problem-solve, to meet each other's needs.

One afternoon I found Anne pulling insulation out from behind the fireplace frame, despite my repeated admonitions to stop. After the third time I'd told her no and she continued, I put her in her highchair for a time-out, turning the high chair toward the wall. She was there about 30 seconds before she called, in twin-speak, for aid. Grant looked up from the end table where he was straining to reach the TV remote, then charged in on a toy car to rescue her. He put a toy phone on her highchair tray for her entertainment, and pushed the highchair, sister and all, away from the wall. Then, as I stood, entranced, unable to believe what I was seeing, he clung to the front of her chair, and they talked in twin speak.

Surely part of the problem was feeling like Jane Goodall in my own home. My instincts ran to observation rather than intervention, preferring to grab a notebook and jot down details about how the twins interacted. It began even before they were born, this delicate dance between the two, and it has always been mesmerizing. I spent hours watching my belly undulate as they swam inside it, never dreaming I'd one day do the same with the babies, toddlers, then children living in my home.

Fascinating or not, the twin speak was a real problem. At 18 months our pediatrician referred us to a developmental specialist. The evaluation process was long and involved, culminating in a diagnosis of a speech delay. The specialist put a number on it, telling us that both children were approximately 33% behind where they should be. My anxiety and guilt kicked into high gear, flashing back to the dozens of ultrasounds and all the medicine to stop contractions and prevent pre-term labor. The doctors assured me it was safe, but what if it somehow damaged the babies? Mark gently pointed out that had they been born three months early, their speech delay would no doubt be worse, and the least of our problems.

We started speech therapy once a week with Peggy. I was initially concerned that her northern accent (she pronounced "orange" as "ornge") would rub off on the kids, but she assured me that the kids would sound every bit as southern as their parents.

Four months into speech therapy the twins learned to say some words, but pulling English from them felt like dragging a couple of particularly reticent mules along for a Sunday stroll. They continued to use twin speak with each other, and the cryptophasia defied our best efforts at decryption. Eventually, I identified one word: "tu-tu" was "milk." But "tu-tu" was not our Nell moment; it didn't crack the code to their whole world, and we all remained maddeningly mute to each other.

Eventually, Grant and Anne were discharged from speech therapy, having hit some invisible metric that pronounced them sufficiently caught up. But they still lagged behind other children their age, and I worried. They expressed a preference for each other over anyone else, which made sense, given that they were the only two people with whom they could communicate.

When Grant and Anne were two and a half, we enrolled them in preschool two mornings a week. I was a bit nervous, but figured that together, they would be fine, even if they couldn't talk to anyone else.

One month after they started preschool, there was no sign of their speech delay. The conversations in the backseat of the van drifted from cryptic mumbo-jumbo to typical toddler fare. Twin speak faded into the ether quietly, with a whimper. I find myself wistful in retrospect, wishing for a recording of the speech that is now only a memory. Would they understand it now? Would they recognize their secrets? Do they still hold a key?

In the end, what it took to conquer twin speak was not the months of speech therapy—though I'm sure that was helpful—or all the time I took to work with them myself. No, what it took to inspire them to speak as we did was providing compelling reasons to do so. Reasons that took the shape of a classroom full of new potential friends, none of who knew one iota of twin speak.

Most twins do not develop twin speak. No one can tell us for sure why our children did, but our pediatrician's best guess is that it has something to do with the closeness of their relationship. It's not something for which we can take any credit. They were so closely bonded from birth that the hospital nursery staff decided, after one memorable (and loud) incident, for the sake of the other babies in the nursery, never to separate ours again. The nurses started putting them to sleep in the same bassinet, and at home they shared a Moses basket, then a crib, and, finally, a bedroom.

No matter where we placed them in a crib, they found each other. They burrowed into one another, and if their arms were free of swaddling blankets, they held hands. They slept nestled together, foreheads touching, almost always facing. It was the stuff dreamy photographs are made of, until we noticed that one side of their heads was starting to flatten from the constant pressure.

At four and a half months, the pediatrician insisted that we put the babies into separate cribs, lest they accidentally hurt each other while they slept. They cried nonstop for several days. A few months later I walked into their room and found them holding hands through the crib rails. Once they were big enough to get out of their individual cribs, we would find them huddled together in one crib, talking quite seriously. Or, on more interesting days, exploring their ecosystem together. My heart still hasn't recovered from the shock of finding Anne sitting atop a nightstand giggling while Grant tried to climb after her.

Now at eight, while their relationship has evolved, the twins are as close as ever. When I find them curled up together reading, they are inevitably touching. Maybe just a foot or the very tips of their elbows, but touching. Days at school are spent in separate classes, so afternoons and evenings they catch up on all they missed. When they are apart for any length of time, there is a sense of held breath, of mental cataloging of things from menial to miracle. They hold space for each other whether or not they are presently together. Though I can understand their speech now, I remain an outsider in the relationship, superfluous. When I am truly struggling to understand something about one twin, the quickest path to understanding is not necessarily to talk to the child in question, but to the other twin. Usually, they know each other better than themselves.

Twin speak had a huge impact on our lives for a relatively short period, and Grant and Anne don't even remember it now. They see it as a bizarre story about how they used to call milk "tu-tu," a story that still makes Mommy oddly nostalgic. They are too close to their own relationship to appreciate the beauty of it, the magic of having another half to meet under the bed for a heart-to-heart in the middle of the day. If twin speak is a result of the particular closeness they have, it was worth every bit of worry and stress. I've never seen anything as beautiful as the relationship my twins share, and my hope is that it will be theirs for life.

Angie Kinghorn is a freelance writer who has published pieces on Good Housekeeping, Redbook, BonBon Break, *and* In the Powder Room. *Her work is published in five anthologies, including the best-selling humor compilation* You Have Lipstick on Your Teeth. *She was a BlogHer VOTY honoree in 2012.*

THE FIRST YEARS

STORYTIME, INTERRUPTED

SUSAN MOLDAW

I started reading to my triplet sons when they were 18 months. Post-dinner and post-baths, the boys bounded into my bedroom, wearing clean, cotton, printed pajamas, their hair smelling sweetly of shampoo, their faces scrubbed and bright. We gathered round on the carpeted floor and I read them little age-appropriate cardboard books with drawings of contented cows, baby chicks, and ducklings bedding down for sleep. My sons quietly listened as they chewed pages, patted bunny tails and sniffed chocolate lollypops in the other thick-paged books I'd scattered about. I wanted them to love reading as much as I did.

When they were 20 months, they lost interest. While I was trying to read, they would jump up and down and yell and laugh obnoxiously, screaming at each other.

"My turn!"

"I want the book!"

"No, me!"

I bought three of every book so each boy could hold one as we read.

One night, feeling grim, I began to read. The savage three nestled on my king-size bed and soon another fight erupted. Who got Mommy's lap? Who sat to her right? To her left? Who chose the book?

A round of "Eeny Meeny Miny Moe" assuaged one squall, but rock-paper-scissors ended in a fight. By the time we began to read again, I was champing at the bit to get them off my hands and into bed.

Suddenly the one on my left couldn't see! And the one on my lap was blocking the one on my right! The third boy jumped off my bed and scampered across the room. I flung *The Runaway Bunny* against the wall. It bounced off, landing in a tent on the floor.

"Go to bed!" I yelled.

The kids stopped their gyrations and stared at me. Then one started to laugh and soon another one did and then they were all giggling and jumping from my bed to the floor and back again.

It was all I could do to keep from screaming, throwing more books, or strong-arming them into submission, but my better self said, *Whoa! Who's the grown-up? Start modeling appropriate behavior!* I struggled for composure.

Then the proverbial light bulb flashed. For all their bleary-eyed complaining, mothers of one child had something we mothers of twins and triplets rarely had unless we planned: one-on-one time. Why couldn't I take a page from their book? Time to divide and conquer my unruly mob.

I scooted off the bed, picked up *The Runaway Bunny*, and laid it on the nightstand. Scooping up two kicking, squirming renegades, I hauled them to their separate rooms and snapped their child gates shut. I did the same with the third. From the hall I could see them all standing like tiny prisoners.

"That's it," I said. "From now on I'll read to each of you in your rooms by yourselves."

"No!" They howled en masse.

"Me first!"

"Why?"

I watched their tear-streaked faces and felt like howling along. I longed for us to be one cuddly group tearing through children's classics, but fantasy didn't match reality. It never had. My dream of easily getting pregnant, glowing pregnancy, natural childbirth, and breastfeeding had morphed into fertility drugs, 10 weeks of home and hospital bed rest, a planned Caesarean, and bottles all the way. I'd learned to roll with the punches.

"That's life, kids," I said.

Every night after that, I padded from room to room and sat beside each tucked-in son. We snuggled. I held the book and read, pointing to words and pictures, answering questions, and talking. Sometimes I went slowly and sometimes fast, according to each son's desires. My words, my laughter, my closeness were all for that boy, and his for me. So we bonded. After a few nights of grumbling, they got to like our time alone. Each waited patiently in bed for his turn, making only an occasional peep. So what if I sometimes read the same story three times in a row and the stack of unread novels by my bed grew taller?

It was worth it.

Susan Moldaw works as a chaplain in San Francisco. Her work has appeared in Brain, Child, Lilith, Literary Mama, Narrative, *and other publications. She is the mother of triplets.*

THE FIRST YEARS

SIDE BY SIDE

_____

ALLIE SMITH

I was alone when I found that I was pregnant with twins. My husband was out of town, and I didn't want to tell him the big news over the phone. It was hard to keep the secret, and I _may_ have told one or two or 20 people before him. But I had to see his reaction in person. I'll never forget the look on his face when I showed him the image from my ultrasound— his eyes nearly fell out of his head.

Having twins is pretty cool. Once the shock of the news wears off, there's the experience and excitement of telling everyone. Reactions are priceless and usually followed by lots of questions. So many questions. Are they identical or fraternal? Boys, girls, or one of each? There are endless queries about names. People are obsessed with twin names. Should the names begin with the same letter? Should the names rhyme? Or be completely different? Maybe Twin A's name could start with an A and Twin B's with a B? Fashion becomes paramount to friends and family. Will we dress them alike or simply coordinate? Or should we designate certain colors for each twin? Would they sleep in the same bed? Or separate cribs? Same room or separate?

I was already familiar with twin excitement and curiosity. One of my closest friends from high school is the mother of identical twin boys. I fell in love with them; I couldn't get enough. As much as I enjoyed those gorgeous boys, I knew first-hand they were a lot of work. I was more than happy to hand them off to their parents when it got to be too much. On a regular basis, I'd declare that I hoped I didn't have twins one day. Surprise, surprise!

I'm the mother of identical twin boys. For the record, we decided on entirely different names but went alphabetically. Twin A was named Barrett, and Twin B, Hunter. We decided to dress them differently, despite the fact that we received several identical outfits. If there was a blue outfit, it was usually worn by Barrett because of the B. And if there was a green one it went to Hunter, because of "hunter green." We thought we were so clever. The boys slept in separate cribs, but in the same room. Always the same room. Even when they were in the NICU and the "feed and grow" nursery at the hospital, they were in the same room, their incubators side by side. That's how I thought it would always be—Barrett and Hunter side by side.

Having had the opportunity to see my friend's twins grow up, I assumed my boys would behave in the same ways. My friend's boys were very much alike and shared the same tastes and interests. They participated in the same activities, were in the same class at school, and had the same friends. They also shared the same bedroom and liked it. The twin force was strong with those two.

We had an unusual situation. Our boys suffered from twin to twin transfusion syndrome in the womb, which necessitated a premature delivery. As a result, the boys had significant developmental delays. By the time they were four, it was apparent my boys were on different paths. Barrett had autism. Hunter was initially diagnosed with Pervasive Development Delay, but fortunately, he quickly responded to early intervention. Hunter talked; Barrett did not. Hunter played with toys; Barrett did not. Hunter went to school with typical children; Barrett did not.

Even with Barrett's autism, the boys had a bond, and I believed sharing a room helped strengthen their connection. I loved hearing their harmonious giggles erupt over the baby monitor. Their cohabitation also made Barrett feel safe. More than once, when they were babies, I would find that Barrett had climbed out of his crib and into his brother's.

As Barrett and Hunter got older, though, I worried about them being roomies. By the time Barrett was a toddler, he had trouble falling asleep. He'd be up for hours after we put him to bed. By comparison, Hunter appreciated and needed sleep. When the Sandman came calling, Hunter would drop wherever he was and fall asleep. Several times I found him sound asleep on the stairs. I was concerned that Barrett's nocturnal habits would affect Hunter. It would not be unusual to find Barrett at 3 a.m. with all the lights on and stuffed animals and books strewn all over the floor. It wasn't fair to his twin.

When the boys were four, we moved. While construction on our new home was in the process of completion, we rented a small apartment. Apartment living was an adjustment, especially with a high-strung child who didn't deal well with change. The situation was tough on the boys because most of their toys and all of the furniture and bedding was in storage. In those cramped quarters, I had many long nights with Barrett.

We'd often visit the house to check on progress. Our new home had five bedrooms, which meant the boys could each have a room of their own. Separating them had become a necessity. Hunter was thrilled by this. Every time we'd go to the house, he'd climb the stairs, counting the steps as he went. He'd sprint to his room, declaring that he couldn't wait to have a room all of his own. Barrett, his ever-devoted twin, would follow him. Hunter didn't appreciate this and made it quite clear to his brother that it was *his* room. Then he'd forcibly turn his brother around and lead him to the room next door saying, "This is *your* room, Barrett." He even wagged his finger in Barrett's face a few times.

In the new home, Dad would ask Hunter if he was scared to sleep by himself. Hunter insisted that he wasn't, but conceded that Barrett might be. I asked him, "Aren't you worried about your twin?" He emphatically replied, "Nope." I didn't appreciate his apathetic attitude.

I was proud of Hunter and all that he had achieved. I was grateful that he had a bright future and tried not to let his brother's struggles overshadow his achievements. I didn't want Barrett to hold Hunter back. But I was also sad because I couldn't help but feel that he was leaving Barrett behind. I couldn't help but wonder if Barrett was feeling it too. But my Bear seemed unaffected by it all, and that made me sad as well.

Our first day in the new house was a long one. Moving is never fun, especially with three kids—one who was a baby and one who had special needs. When it was time for bed, I didn't have to coax Hunter. He was so excited to sleep in his new room for the first time. After I kissed him goodnight, he couldn't get me out of there fast enough. I asked, "Are you sure you're not nervous about sleeping by yourself?" With an uncharacteristic cockiness, he assured me that he was not.

As I was tucking Barrett into bed, I tried to explain that this was his room, and he was a big boy. I didn't address the reasons for the separation. "Hunter still loves you Barrett, and he's only next door." I assured him that everything was all right, and said if he got scared he could find me. He didn't say anything, only smiled. He wiggled under the covers of his red and blue quilt, which he'd been without for three months. Worried and feeling guilty, I read him an extra book before kissing him goodnight.

I turned off his bedside light, and the room took on a soft glow from the lighthouse nightlight. I lingered, stole a few more cuddles and kisses. It was then that I heard the creak of the bathroom door that connected Barrett and Hunter's rooms. I looked up from where I was lying on the bed, and was able to see through the bathroom mirror that the door had indeed opened.

A small voice traveled through the door, a voice that sounded more than a little nervous, "Barrett? Bear-Bear, are you in there?"

This was about to get interesting. I quickly lay back down next to Bear, but with my head propped up on his pillow, so I could still see the mirror. I could see the top of Hunter's little head as he crept around the corner.

His shaky voice continued from the vanity alcove, "Barrett are you still awake?" He approached the bed, tiptoeing, "Are you okay in here Barrett?"

I couldn't contain my laughter any longer and popped up declaring, "Busted!"

A startled Hunter jumped a foot in the air.

I couldn't stop laughing, and even Barrett understood the hilarity of the situation, joining me in laughter. A red-faced Hunter fumbled his excuse, "I was just checking on him." Given all his bravado about being on his own, and his nonchalance about his twin, I doubted it. And he didn't offer any further explanation, just turned on his heel and fled back from where he came.

Once I regained my composure, I visited Hunter and gave him an extra tuck-in, making sure not to laugh.

There were more than a couple of slumber parties over the years. Ten years later, we're in a new house, and the boys are once again sharing a room. Ironically, it's now Barrett who goes to sleep early and Hunter's the night owl. Hunter's late-night studying and Internet surfing do not seem to affect Barrett. I believe having his twin close is all Barrett needs to sleep these days, especially if his brother tucks him in. I just hope Hunter's future wife is okay with their arrangement!

Allie Smith is a freelance writer and blogger who writes about parenting, autism, books, and travel on her blog, The Latchkey Mom. *She's an assistant editor for The HerStories Project and a contributing book reviewer for Chick Lit Plus. Each summer, she takes an epic road trip with four children and documents their adventures in a monthly column for* My Forsyth *magazine. Her work has been published by the* Huffington Post, Scary Mommy, Full Grown People, The Forsyth Herald, Club Mid, Autism Speaks, *and various other sites. Most recently, Allie had an essay included in the anthology,* Mothering Through the Darkness.

MUST-HAVE BABY ACCESSORIES FOR MULTIPLES

MEGAN WOOLSEY

When you're are a parent of multiples, there are certain decisions, concessions, sacrifices and compromises that need to be made when it comes to buying baby things. It is not always financially possible, nor practical, to have multiples of the same baby items.

When my triplets were born, many people donated their baby swings, vibrating seats, activity mats and so on to my family in an effort to help us through that first year. Sometimes having only one or two of an item would suffice with multiples, and other times I needed to make a trip to Babies R Us for that extra item so each baby would have their own.

I only had two Boppy pillows, which seemed like plenty. In reality, the Boppy pillow was the most important baby accessory we owned. Each baby needed their own Boppy to cozy up inside of. The Boppy not only helped prop the babies up for breastfeeding, they were also instrumental in providing the perfect position for them to lay in when I needed a safe and comfortable place for them while I did things around the house.

As a new mom, it is going to be invaluable to have some free time to do chores or rest. You do not need to buy multiples of everything on the list below, but it is important that you choose some of these items to have more than one

191

of. It is always a possibility to buy one ExerSaucer, one swing, and one activity mat and rotate the babies through them, like a circuit training course.

Here are some options for helpful accessories that you may need one for each baby:

- Bobby pillows

- Swings, such as the Rock 'n Play Sleeper

- High chairs

- Bouncers

- Activity mats

- Bumbo seats

- Cribs

- ExerSaucers

- Push walkers

- Baba Buddy, or other hands-free bottle holders

- Pacifier clips to attach them to clothing

- Swaddling blankets and/or Halo Sleep Sacks (mine were so invaluable to me that I still have the ones my triplets used as keepsakes)

- Mobiles

- Pack 'N Plays

- Diaper pails

  Awesome products made exclusively for parents with multiples:

- Twin Z Nursing pillow or My Brest Friend

- Twin baby carrier

- Graco Pack 'n Play with twin bassinet

- Twins shopping cart cover

- Double swim float

- Feeding and activity tables for twins, triplets and more

- Baby Trend Double Snap-N-Go

- Table For Two feeding system for feeding two babies at once

There are many products available for new babies today; it is difficult to know which ones are right for you and your multiples. Not all of these items will suit your children, and some will be a lifesaver. This list of favorites should help ease your babies' transition into the world.

JOURNAL IT

Write your thoughts and feelings down. Capture the moments. Life with multiples is exciting and busy, and it's easy to forget the little things and details. Here are some writing prompts to help you along.

Write down your biggest success story so far as a parent of multiples.

Write down a moment where your twins/triplets/more said or did something that was laugh out loud funny.

HELPFUL TIPS FOR SURVIVING AND THRIVING DURING THE FIRST YEAR WITH MULTIPLES

EDITORS AND CONTRIBUTORS

"In the middle of it all, when things are falling through the cracks, your priorities have all tumbled together, the floor is covered in puffs and baby drool, you are exhausted, and you wonder if you are doing it right—know that you are."

Jackie Pick

"Ask for help and then take it, early and often."

Allie Capo-Burdick

"Find other parents of multiples to hang out with (either in person or online). They are the only people on the planet who can totally relate to what you are going through."

Ellen Nordberg

"Create a plan for organization before your multiples are born, because it will help keep your sanity intact. We created a spreadsheet so we could record feeding, sleeping and potty schedules so we didn't accidentally feed someone twice and starve someone else. My mother-in-law likes to share with everyone that the key to my success in caring for infant triplets is my ability to stay organized."

Megan Woolsey

"Write everything down. You will forget what you need to do on a regular basis. Also, keep a notebook to write down everything your kids say and do. Get your multiples on a sleep schedule early on. Let go of all expectations and you will enjoy your babies so much more."

Lexi Rohner

"There will be many times when you are overwhelmed—feeling outnumbered, exhausted, covered in vomit, ready to cry and not knowing what to do next. Take a breath and appreciate the absurdity and humor of your unique situation. It will get easier, and if you can laugh about it, you can get through your day."

Shanna Silva

"Learn how to use your feet as a second set of hands."

Briton Underwood

"Embrace the chaos. Life with twins isn't easy, and it's never boring. What I've learned in four long (short) years: Don't underestimate the horror of potty training times two, stay in the moment as much as you can (which I realize is an oxymoron with multiples because you have to constantly plan ahead), and always have snacks on hand. Lots of snacks for them, but some for you too (chocolate covered espresso beans, anyone?)."

Amy Paturel

"Remind yourself that every phase in the life of your multiples has a beginning and an end. You may as well laugh during your kids' current crazy phase, because it will soon be over, but rest assured that the next phase will likely be a doozy!"

Kirsten Gant

"It's easy to compare your multiples because they are the same age. Don't. Each child is different. One will walk sooner than the other. One will love solids, the other, not so much. One will talk earlier. You will feel affinity with one more than the other, and with which child changes daily! It's totally normal. Accept that they are individuals despite the fact that they shared a womb."

Alison Lee

"Shake yourself from the haze of exhaustion and be present in every moment. I can't remember one thing about my twins the first year. If I hadn't photographed and videotaped them so much, I would have forgotten who they were."

Shelly Stolaroff Segal

"Take care of yourself. Take breaks. Go out by yourself—call a friend, hire a babysitter, take a nap, ask for help."

Susan Moldaw

"One-on-one time with each child is special for parents and children."

Becki Melchione

"Don't be afraid to ask for help. Remember that everything is a phase, and you will get through each stage. And here's something specific and practical: If you had an extra big belly, get checked for a diastasis in your ab muscles."

Janet McNally

"Beyond about a year, don't dress your babies alike. As they get older, encourage friends not to give them matching outfits. It may look cute to you and others, but dressing them differently is one of the easiest ways you can give your multiples their individual identities."

MeiMei Fox

"While you can do it on your own, there is no need to. Don't feel bad about relying on your family and friends for help. If ever anyone offers you help (a night off, making meals, mowing your lawn) take them up on it. Make a list of offers, and follow up on it. If the offers for help aren't coming, don't be too proud to ask them for help."

Jared Bond

"Label all baby pictures. You think that you'll remember who's who, but you won't. I had my twins in the dark ages of film, and whenever I got the pictures back, I'd write on the back of each picture who it was. I did this for pictures I was mailing out to family and friends as well. Now, when I go through old albums, the kids will ask me, "Is that Barrett or Hunter?" Most of the time I have to pull the picture out and look at the back! I even do it now, with digital photos. They each have a computer file for their individual pictures."

Allie Smith

"Leave your house regularly. It feels impossible sometimes, especially in the early days, but do it. Whether you have to figure out how to fold your tandem stroller or how to wrap the babies on your body, know that it is a skill like anything else to go out with your babies, and practice makes it easier each time. Don't stay home because you're afraid they will cry. They probably will, but at least you get to see some of the world instead of all your unfolded laundry."

Melanie Sweeney

"Keep an eye on your own mental health and seek help immediately if you start to experience signs of postpartum depression. Mothers of multiples are almost <u>twice as likely</u> as mothers of singletons to experience postpartum depression. Talk to your partner before you give birth about the possibility of postpartum depression or other postpartum mood disorders, and ask him to observe you after the babies are born. It is not an easy thing for a partner to do, but he may need to tell you if he sees that you need help; my husband did. Develop a plan for what you will do if you need help. Don't assume that this won't happen to you. It might not, but if it does, managing it will be much easier with a plan in place."

Angie Kinghorn

"Someone once gave me a tip about what to say to the people who thoughtlessly say, "It's so much work! Don't you ever wish there was just one?" Her advice was to say, "I never wished there was one of them, but I often wish there were two of me.""

Janine Kovac

ACKNOWLEDGEMENTS

It isn't every day that we get the opportunity to follow our dreams and turn blank pages into a beautiful book.

Thank you to the most loving and supportive husband a girl could ever hope for. Chris is not only the best dad to triplets and their big sister, but he is also my tech support and editor.

To my beautiful children whom I love with all my heart: whether you wanted to be or not, you are my muses. I have you to thank for being the inspiration I needed to keep writing.

I am fortunate to have family and friends who keep me smiling and lift me up when I need support: mom, dad, Sherri, Richard, Molly, Nima, Sarah, Lea – love you.

Thank you to my partner and friend, Alison. Your ability to keep us organized and on task has been instrumental. The process of writing and editing this book with you has been an absolute pleasure.

Thank you, Susan Pinsky, for lending your pen to write the foreword of this book—we are grateful and honored to have you. I am immensely proud of this book and all of the remarkable writers who help fill the pages.

~ *Megan Woolsey*

When I first told my husband that I was going to be editing a book about twins, triplets and more with a fellow multiples mother who lives halfway across the world, he said, "Great idea. Do it." He says that for many, if not all, of my

AWKNOWLEDGEMENTS

projects, no matter how wild they sound. There is no way I could have done this without his support and belief in me. Thank you, my love.

To my four wonderful, amazing children: my boys who taught me about mothering and prepared me for the twins who set me on this path - I love you to the moon and beyond.

Thank you to the various people who made this book possible: our contributors, beta readers, blurb writers, and Susan Pinsky, who wrote a terrific foreword. We appreciate the time and effort you put into this project.

And to Megan, my partner in this crazy and amazing ride—thank you for saying yes and putting your trust in me. Look at this baby we've birthed!

~ Alison Lee

ABOUT THE EDITORS

Megan Woolsey and Alison Lee are writers and mothers of multiples (triplets and twins, respectively). Together they are publishing this first ever anthology all about multiples. The book is comprised of original essays from Megan, Alison and guest writers, as well as tips and advice about raising multiples, from infertility and labor pains through the first few years. Our vision is to bring together the world of multiples through shared stories.

Parents of multiples have a unique bond that ties us together. Our hope is that readers will find value and entertainment connecting with parents of multiples and learning about their journey.

Megan Woolsey is a writer, editor and publisher living in Northern California with a very supportive husband and a wild bunch of red-headed children - a set of triplets and their big sister. Megan has been published in Huffington Post, Scary Mommy, BLUNTmoms, Bonbon Break, Mamalode, In The Powder Room and is an essayist in two anthologies. She began writing professionally for her blog, The Hip Mothership, which she began while in the hospital eating copious amounts of Jell-O on bed rest pregnant with triplets. When Megan isn't busy writing or blogging, she loves hot yoga, long walks, and dinner with friends that includes good bottles of wine.

ABOUT THE EDITORS

Alison Lee is a writer, editor and publisher. A former PR and marketing professional, she is the owner of Little Love Media, specializing in blog book tours. Alison's writing has been featured in Mamalode, On Parenting at The Washington Post, The Huffington Post, Everyday Family, Scary Mommy, and Club Mid. She is one of 35 essayists in the anthology, *My Other Ex: Women's True Stories of Leaving and Losing Friends* (Fall, 2014), and has an essay in another, *So Glad They Told Me: Women Get Real About Motherhood* (Spring, 2016). She is also an editor at BonBon Break, an online magazine. Alison lives in Malaysia with her husband and four children (two boys and boy/ girl twins).

MORE INFORMATION

Visit the Multiples Illuminated website:
www.multiplesilluminated.com

Email Multiples Illuminated:
multiplesilluminated@gmail.com

Like Multiples Illuminated on Facebook:
www.facebook.com/MultiplesIlluminated

Tweet Multiples Illuminated on Twitter:
www.twitter.com/MultiplesIllum

Pin with Multiples Illuminated on Pinterest:
www.pinterest.com/MultiplesIllum

Visit the Multiples Illuminated Zazzle store:
www.zazzle.com/multiplesilluminated

MORE INFORMATION

MULTIPLES RESOURCES

Multiples of America (aka National Organization of Mothers of Twins Clubs (NOMTC)

The Multiples of America aka NOMOTC is a 501(c)(3) non-profit organization dedicated to supporting families of multiple birth children through support, education, research. Multiples of America promotes support and networking for parents of multiples. Opportunities for self-help, emotional support and parenting information are provided through local club and state organization meetings.

Twins Magazine

TWINS™ Magazine is the premiere magazine for parents of multiples, from twins and triplets to quadruplets, quintuplets and more! Published bi-monthly or six times each year, TWINS™ Magazine is the "bible of parenting multiples," loved by moms and dads of twins and higher-order multiples since 1984.

Twiniversity

Now reaching almost 100,000 families in over 150 countries, Twiniversity is the largest global resource for all things "twinnie". With worldwide recognition in her field, Natalie Diaz brings her twin parenting expertise to their online resource and parent-to-parent forums.

Twins Doctor

Launched in 2007, TwinsDoctor.com is the first physician-authored website to provide health information exclusively for multiples.

Babies in Belly

Babies in Belly offers convenient, virtual prenatal classes taught by a certified teacher and mother of monozygotic twin boys.

Raising Multiples

Raising Multiples was founded as MOST (Mothers of Supertwins) in 1987 by a community of families, volunteers and professionals. They are the leading national nonprofit provider of support, education and research on higher-order multiple births.

Twin Pregnancy and Beyond

It was lovingly founded by a mother of twins in 2007 on the basis of offering the best and most up-to-date "twin specific" information and support on all aspects of twins - from finding out about your twin pregnancy, through twin birth, raising twins and beyond.

The Twin to Twin Transfusion Syndrome Foundation

The Twin to Twin Transfusion Syndrome Foundation is the first and only international nonprofit organization solely dedicated to providing immediate and lifesaving educational, emotional and financial support to families, medical professionals and other caregivers before, during and after a diagnosis of twin to twin transfusion syndrome.

Twins Day Festival

The Twins Days Festival is the largest annual gathering of twins and multiples in the world and takes place every August in Twinsburg, Ohio. It's open to all twins and multiples, young and old.

Twins Online

A helpful and informative site loaded with topics covering all aspects of twins.

Centre for the Study of Multiple Birth

This non-profit organization was founded in 1977 by identical twins, Louis and Donald Keith to promote research, education, and public service for multiple births.

Dad's Guide to Twins

A dad's guide to all things twins, including finance how to raise healthy babies, tips for physically caring for two, getting twins to sleep, and more.

KellyMom

This is one of the most comprehensive websites for moms, and was developed to provide evidence-based information on breastfeeding and parenting. Kelly is the mother of three lovely children, and an International Board Certified Lactation Consultant (IBCLC).

New Mommy Media

Based in San Diego, New Mommy Media is a network of dynamic audio podcasts. Their shows give tips and advice for new parents, educating and entertaining moms and dads as they transition into parenthood. Each 30-minute episode features everyday parents and experts discussing relevant issues in a relaxed, roundtable format, and they have a weekly podcast called *Twin Talks*.

Joan A. Friedman, Ph.D

Dr. Friedman is a prominent and well-respected twin expert who shares her passionate views and insights about twins and their emotional needs with twins and their families throughout the world. The fact that she is an identical twin and the mother of five, including fraternal twin sons, makes her ideally suited to this task. Her commitment to twin research and her treatment of twins of all ages demonstrate the breadth and depth of her skills and experience.

Twinless Twins Support Group

This organization provides a safe and compassionate community for twinless twins to experience healing and understanding. They also provide support for twins and other multiples who have lost their twin due to death or estrangement at any age.

CPSIA information can be obtained
at www.ICGtesting.com
Printed in the USA
FSHW012319080119
54899FS

9 780996 833509